And some comments from parents

'Thank you! I read this book believing it was for my own interest but what I discovered was that many issues were extremely relevant and useful in our "normal"… family. The dialogues really made sense and gave such good examples of how to talk to your children, how to draw them out and get to the bottom of their problems… I think this book will be of huge benefit to parents, teachers and healthcare professionals who come into contact with shy and socially anxious children.'

Mrs E., Carmarthenshire

'Although primarily designed for parents and children suffering with problematic anxiety, I think it would help anyone dealing with children … The ways of talking to the child and guiding them through their own thought processes and feelings are really enlightening.'

Mrs F., Ceridigion

'[*Overcoming Your Child's Shyness and Social Anxiety*] is both informative and helpful. Each chapter is easy to read and understand. It will be brilliant for any parent with an anxious or shy child to use as a reference book. The case histories are extremely useful as the examples often remind us of situations we have found ourselves in. This reassured us as we now realize that our daughter's anxiety and shyness are not unique. We would definitely recommend this book to other families that find themselves in the same situation. Owning a copy of this book will be like having a counsellor in your own home.'

Mr and Mrs V., Berkshire

'[This book] provides a very clear insight into the child's experience of anxiety which is easy to overlook when parents are experiencing high levels of frustration …[It is] extremely readable and very user-friendly. The attention to detail… makes the steps in this book as easy as they can be to implement in hectic family life. I liked the fact that many of the issues covered in the book would be of benefit to all parents whether their children are anxious or not.'

Mrs C., Berkshire

'This book is an invaluable and extremely practical self-help guide. It offers a clear, step-by-step approach to help parents and children build confidence and develop effective coping strategies for everyday challenges. As a parent of a socially anxious child, I found that this book offers a very accessible approach. I cannot imagine a family who could not gain some benefit from reading this book.'

Mrs Z., Woking

Praise for *Overcoming Your Child's Fears and Worries* by Cathy Creswell and Lucy Willetts

'I think Cathy Creswell and Lucy Willetts should be congratulated on writing such an accessible yet comprehensive and informative book. They pitch the book at the right level for parents and professionals alike – compassionate and non-judgemental without skimping on the hard facts of the biological, psychological and social realities of these issues. I read it in one sitting and felt I had learnt a lot by the end. I loved the no-nonsense, practical approach that will be an empowering relief to parents, themselves paralysed by the anxiety of their own child's anxieties. Feel a bit jealous that I didn't write it myself!'

Dr. Tanya Byron, Consultant Clinical Psychologist on the House of Tiny Tearaways, BBC TV

'This excellent book is very well written and is essential reading for any parent who is concerned that their child is anxious. At the outset it provides information to help parents understand the nature of children's fears or concerns, how they develop, and why they persist. It also helps parents to distinguish between what are common and "ordinary" fears and worries, and what kinds of worries might require some form of parental intervention. The book reads very easily and parents would do well to have a copy on their bookshelves to enable them to dip into it at times of stress.'

Alan Stein, Professor of Child and Adolescent Psychiatry, University of Oxford

'This book is a very thorough and detailed practical guide ... which will be very useful for both therapists working with children with fears and worries as well as families who are able to use this book as a "self-help" treatment guide.'

Dr Penny Titman, Consultant Clinical Psychologist, Great Ormond Street Hospital

'Being frightened and worrying too much of the time gets in the way of children and teenagers playing, having fun together, and getting on with their education ... Cathy Creswell and Lucy Willetts have done a great job in making this self-help guide for children, teenagers and parents; explaining in a clear and practical way how therapy is done and how it can be done by families themselves.'

Professor Derek Bolton, Anxiety Clinic for Children and Adolescents, South London and Maudsley NHS Trust

The aim of the **Overcoming** series is to enable people with a range of common problems and disorders to take control of their own recovery program. Each title, with its specially tailored program, is devised by a practising clinician using the latest techniques of cognitive behavioral therapy – techniques which have been shown to be highly effective in changing the way patients think about themselves and their problems.

The series was initiated in 1993 by Peter Cooper, Professor of Psychology at Reading University and Research Fellow at the University of Cambridge in the UK whose original volume on overcoming bulimia nervosa and binge-eating continues to help many people in the USA, the UK and Europe. Many books in the Overcoming series are recommended by the UK Department of Health under the Books on Prescription scheme.

All titles in the series are available by mail order.
Please see the order form at the back of this book.
www.overcoming.co.uk

OVERCOMING YOUR CHILD'S SHYNESS & SOCIAL ANXIETY

A self-help guide using
Cognitive Behavioral Techniques

Lucy Willetts & Cathy Creswell

ROBINSON
London

Constable & Robinson Ltd
3 The Lanchesters
162 Fulham Palace Road
London W6 9ER
www.constablerobinson.com

First published in the UK by Robinson,
an imprint of Constable & Robinson Ltd 2007

A copy of the British Library Cataloguing in
Publication Data is available from the British Library.

Important Note
This book is not intended as a substitute for medical advice or treatment. Any person with a condition requiring medical attention should
consult a qualified medical practitioner or suitable therapist.

ISBN 978-1-84529-087-0

Printed and bound in the EU

1 3 5 7 9 10 8 6 4 2

Contents

Contents

Acknowledgements

We would like to thank all those whose research we have learned from over the past ten years, in particular Paula Barrett, Deborah Beidel, Vanessa Cobham and Ronald Rapee. Their work has equipped us with a wealth of knowledge and skills that we have applied to our work with children with social anxiety and subsequently to this book.

We would also like to offer our thanks to Professors Peter Cooper and Lynne Murray who have both been an inspiration to us and have supported and helped us in the development of our anxiety clinic and in the writing of this book.

We thank the families of all those children with social anxiety who have been assessed and treated within our clinic. Both the children and parents have taught us a lot and have shown us that with motivation and persistence even very severe social anxiety problems can be overcome.

Finally, we would like to thank our own families, Andrew, Jos and Charlie, Colin and Joe, for their support and understanding as we embarked on and completed this new literary adventure.

Preface

Many children experience anxiety or shyness. It is often hard to know what to do for the best when you have a shy or socially anxious child. You have probably found that lots of people will offer you advice, but this is often conflicting, and other resources that you have tried to access, such as looking on the Internet, may have only served to confuse you further by offering you an overwhelming and frequently bewildering array of information.

We have run a specialist childhood anxiety clinic for several years, which aims to give families of children who have anxiety problems, including social anxiety and shyness, clear, simple advice and support about how to help their child. Our clinic is unique in the way it is funded and managed by both the University of Reading and Berkshire Healthcare NHS Trust. In this way, it combines the research expertise of university-based personnel with the knowledge about treatment that NHS clinicians can provide. This book aims to do the same. We have drawn upon up-to-date relevant research and have, we hope, at the same time produced a book that gives you, as parents, a down-to-earth guide to helping your child. In our clinic, we often help children by working through parents, as we have found that this works just as well or even better than working with the children individually. We have used a similar approach in this book.

First, and in response to the question many parents have asked us, 'Why is my child shy or socially anxious?' we have included, in Part One, information about what may have caused or maintained your child's shyness or social anxiety. In this part we also give you a brief overview of what shyness and social anxiety are to help you to decide whether your child does, in fact, have a problem and, if so, to what extent it is causing difficulties for them. The backbone of this book is Part Two, which consists of five steps that you, as a parent, can work through, and encourage your child to work through to overcome their shyness or social anxiety. We have added two additional principles, which are extra techniques that, we have found from experience, will enhance the results that you and your child get from putting our guidelines into practice. Finally, we have included a further section, Part Three, which deals with specific difficulties associated with shyness and social anxiety, in particular refusal to go to school and a reluctance to speak, which need input from both you and your child's school, and relaxation techniques which can be particularly helpful for children with marked physical symptoms of anxiety. We have also written a chapter in this section for your child's teacher, so that they can follow the principles you are using with your child. And throughout the book we have provided you with simple, practical ways of helping your child to become less shy or socially anxious.

We have used the principles in the book in our work with several hundred families, many of whose children suffer from shyness and social anxiety. The great majority of these children have overcome their shyness and social anxiety, and those who have been most successful have been lucky enough to have highly motivated and committed parents. So by choosing to read this book, you, as a parent, have already given your child a head start!

Introduction: Why a cognitive behavioral approach?

The approach which *Overcoming Your Child's Shyness and Social Anxiety* takes, in attempting to help you overcome your child's problems with shyness and social anxiety, is a cognitive behavioral one. You might find a brief account of the history of this form of intervention useful and encouraging. In the 1950s and 1960s a set of therapeutic techniques was developed, collectively termed 'behavior therapy'. These techniques shared two basic features. First, they aimed to remove symptoms (such as anxiety) by dealing with those symptoms themselves, rather than their deep-seated underlying historical causes (traditionally the focus of psychoanalysis, the approach developed by Sigmund Freud and his associates). Second, they used techniques derived from what laboratory psychologists were finding out about the mechanisms of learning, which could potentially be put to the test, or had already been proven to be of practical value. The area where behavior therapy initially proved to be of most value was in the treatment of anxiety disorders, especially specific phobias (such as extreme fear of animals or heights) and agoraphobia, both notoriously difficult to treat using conventional psychotherapies.

After an initial flush of enthusiasm, discontent with behavior therapy grew. There were a number of reasons for this. An important factor was that behavior therapy did not deal with the internal thoughts which were so obviously central to the distress that many patients were experiencing. In particular, behavior therapy proved inadequate when it came to the treatment of depression. In the late 1960s and early 1970s a treatment for depression was developed called 'cognitive therapy'. The pioneer in this enterprise was an American psychiatrist, Professor Aaron T. Beck. Beck developed a theory of depression which emphasized the importance of people's depressed styles of thinking, and on the basis of this theory, he specified a new form of therapy. It would not be an exaggeration to say that Beck's work has changed the nature of psychotherapy, not just for depression but for a range of psychological problems.

The techniques introduced by Beck have been merged with the techniques developed earlier by behavior therapists, to produce a therapeutic approach which has come to be known as 'cognitive behavioral therapy' (CBT). This therapy has been subjected to the strictest scientific testing and has been found to be highly successful for a significant proportion of cases of depression. It has now become clear that specific patterns of disturbed thinking are associated with a wide range of psychological problems, not just depression, and that the treatments which deal with these are highly effective. So, effective cognitive behavioral treatments have been developed for a range of anxiety disorders, such as panic disorder, generalized anxiety disorder, specific phobias, social phobia, obsessive compulsive disorders, and hypochondriasis (health anxiety), as well as for other conditions such as drug addictions, and eating disorders like bulimia nervosa. Indeed, cognitive behavioral techniques have been found to have an application beyond the narrow categories of psychological disorders. They have been applied effectively, for example, to helping people with low self-esteem, people with weight problems, couples with marital difficulties, and those who wish to give up smoking, or deal with drinking problems.

The starting point for CBT is the realization that the way we think, feel and behave are all intimately linked, and changing the way we think about ourselves, our experiences, and the world around us changes the way we feel and what we are able to do. So, for example, by helping a depressed person identify and challenge their automatic depressive thoughts, a route out of the cycle of depressive thoughts and feelings can be found. Similarly, habitual behavioral responses are driven by a complex set of thoughts and feelings, and CBT, as you will discover from this book, by providing a means for the behavior to be brought under cognitive control, enables these responses to be undermined and a different kind of life to be possible.

In recent years, CBT treatments have been developed for children and teenagers and research has produced very encouraging results, especially for the treatment of children's anxiety problems. Often these treatments involve clinicians working with both the child and the child's parent(s); however, working with parents alone, to help them help their child has been found, in some studies, to be just as effective.

Although effective CBT treatments have been developed for a wide range of disorders and problems, these treatments are not widely available, and when people try on their own to help themselves or their children, they often, inadvertently, do things which make matters worse. In recent years the community of cognitive behavioral therapists has responded to this by taking the principles and techniques of CBT for particular problems and presenting them in manuals which people can read and apply themselves. These manuals specify a systematic program of treatment which the reader works through to overcome their difficulties. In this way, cognitive behavioral therapeutic techniques of proven value are being made available on the widest possible basis. The current manual has been written specifically for parents of children with social anxiety and shyness and it provides them with a clear set of therapeutic principles that they can systematically apply to help their children.

Self-help manuals are never going to replace therapists. Many families will need the help of a qualified therapist. It is also the case that, despite the widespread success of cognitive behavioral therapy, some people will not respond to it and will need one of the other treatments available. Although research on the use of these self-help manuals is at an early stage, the work done to date indicates that for a great many people such a manual is sufficient for them to overcome their problems without professional help. Sadly, many families suffer on their own for years. Sometimes they feel reluctant to seek help without first making a serious effort to manage on their own. Sometimes they are ashamed to ask for help. Sometimes appropriate help is not forthcoming despite their efforts to find it. For many of these families the cognitive behavioral self-help manual will provide a lifeline to a better future.

Professor Peter J. Cooper
The University of Reading

Part One

Understanding Your Child's Shyness and Social Anxiety

1

What are shyness and social anxiety?

An introduction to this book

We understand that you are keen to get stuck into the practical parts of this book. However, we urge you to read the next five brief chapters, where we outline what shyness and social anxiety are and what causes them, before moving on to Part Two. There are three important reasons for doing so. First, Chapters 1 and 2 outline what shyness and social anxiety are. By reading these chapters you will be able to make sure that this is the right book for you, in the sense that it will help you to confirm whether your child does experience social anxiety or is shy. Second, Chapter 3 will help you to decide how much of a problem your child's shyness or social anxiety is, and whether now is the right time to be tackling it. Finally, the last two chapters explain how shyness and social anxiety develop in children and what prevents children from growing out of the problem. The information given in these chapters provides the rationale for all the work you will do when you follow the guide in Part Two. Having a clear understanding of why you are following our program will make it much easier for you to put the strategies into effect, and will encourage you to persevere when the going gets tough. A further reason for reading this section is that you will be introduced to five children: Rebecca, Michael, Lauren, Peter and Emily. These children have all been shy or experienced social anxiety, and you will hear some of the background to their difficulties, before reading in Part Two about how their parents helped them to overcome these.

What is shyness?

It is common for children to get anxious about all sorts of things. It is part of growing up and learning about the world. For example, toddlers are often scared of loud noises, while 4- and 5-year-olds are sometimes afraid of monsters or the dark. Young children also commonly get anxious in social situations. As a toddler, it is reasonable for your child to be quiet in situations with people they do not know very well. It is understandable that they might be anxious when they start nursery or school; most children are. They might also be nervous of going to a playgroup or club, or going to a friend's house for tea for the first time. They might be quiet when they meet someone for the first time or with an adult they do not see very often. These behaviors are all normal.

Rebecca is 4 years old and will be starting school soon. Her mum is very worried because Rebecca gets nervous when she is with other people and her mum is concerned that she may find going to school difficult. As a toddler, Rebecca was very quiet and withdrawn at mother and toddler groups and sometimes became upset. When Rebecca was a bit older, her mum took her to a playgroup. Rebecca was painfully shy there and rarely spoke to the helpers or children. She has been there for a year and a half now and does play with two children who she knows well. She will speak to one helper only. Rebecca has always been clingy with her mum. Rebecca's mum has tried to encourage her to mix more by having her close friends round to play and by taking her to ballet class. However, if any of her mum's friends come round for a cup of tea, Rebecca stays very quiet, even though she knows them quite well now. If anyone stops to chat to her mum in the supermarket, she puts her head down or looks away.

Shy children do not get used to these situations, so they almost always feel nervous about one or more social situations, such as going to nursery or school, going to a friend's for tea or talking to adults. They are usually quiet in situations with other people, avoid eye contact, are tense and concerned about the impression they are making on those around them. Shy children are also reluctant to enter into these social situations and will do so with caution and trepidation. They tend to play or spend time alone more than children who are not shy and interact less with their classmates. When they are with other children, for example in the playground, they often stand and watch group activities but do not join in. Children who are shy can also be less assertive than children who are not, in that they are less likely to stick up for themselves or say what they think. They also find it hard to ask teachers or other adults for help. What shy children find most difficult is interacting with people they don't know. In contrast, they can often be chatty and confident at home when they are with their family or close friends.

Michael is 6 years old. He found it hard to settle into school but is happy to attend now. However, he is anxious about using the school toilets and refuses to do so. This sometimes results in him wetting himself while at school. It also means he doesn't drink very much at school so that he can 'hang on' until he gets home. Michael is described as quiet at school and never puts his hand up. He finds working in a group hard and often stands on the sidelines at playtime when the other boys are playing football. Michael does have friends to play with although he usually follows their lead and doesn't say very much. At Michael's request, his parents enrolled him at Beavers, but he now refuses to go and his parents feel that he is missing out on everyday things that children of his age do.

Michael is chatty at home and enjoys spending time with his grandparents and his cousin. He can stay at their houses without any problem and doesn't get upset at being away from his mum and dad at these times.

Although you are probably reading this book because you perceive your child's shyness to be a problem, shyness is sometimes seen as a positive trait. Shy children are often viewed as being rather endearing, particularly in the UK, where being reserved is highly regarded. Shy children are usually well-behaved outside the home, presenting few problems for teachers or other parents, and are commonly considered to be calm and thoughtful, a marked contrast to impulsive or aggressive children. Shyness is more often viewed as a positive trait in girls rather than boys, in whom lively and boisterous behavior is expected. Despite being a positive part of your child's personality, their shyness may also get in the way. For example, many shy children are unable to engage fully in social activities. For these children, their shyness has become a problem, and in this case it is commonly referred to as social anxiety.

What is social anxiety?

Many words are used to describe being anxious, including fearful, scared, nervous or worried. People of all ages experience anxiety. Indeed, all children experience some anxiety and this can, in fact, be quite helpful. Children who are mildly anxious about exams are likely to be more motivated to revise in order to do well, while some anxiety about performance before a school play or sports day can help children to perform better. Anxiety can also be helpful in that it allows us to act quickly if we think we are in danger. For example, if we are crossing the road and see a car coming, our anxiety drives us to get out of the way quickly! For most children, their anxiety is not extreme and does not interfere with their life. Many children, for instance, are afraid of speaking in front of a large group of children or adults, but this does not stop them doing things such as going to school or an after-school club. However some children's anxiety becomes extreme and interferes significantly with their everyday life, and this is when it should be regarded as a problem. So, for example, some children are so scared of speaking in front of others that they will not go to an after-school club, such as Brownies, or in more extreme cases even to school, for fear of having to talk in front of a group of children and adults. Their fear is excessive as it stops these children doing normal things or makes doing them difficult.

Lauren is 9 years old. She is fearful of asking for help in class and answering questions. She hates doing tests for fear of getting a bad mark and often has a headache on these days. Lauren also finds any sort of performance anxiety-provoking, including doing a school play. Lauren has friends at school whom she invites home for tea. She also goes to other children's houses to play and goes to Brownies, but she finds it harder to mix with children she doesn't know well. Lauren says that she is not bothered by her social anxiety. However her mum is worried as she feels that not speaking up in class will cause Lauren a problem when she gets older. She also worries about how Lauren will get on at secondary school where there will be so many children she does not know and she fears that she may be bullied.

Social anxiety is extreme shyness. It is a specific form of anxiety that occurs when a child is in situations with other people, such as going to school, seeing friends and going to restaurants. Children with social anxiety worry that they might do something stupid or embarrassing in these situations, such as saying something silly, which will make other children or adults laugh at them or think negatively about them. As a result, they feel uncomfortable and nervous in situations with other people. This may lead to them being quiet and withdrawn, in the same way as a child who is shy, and some might also become upset or angry. Children who suffer from social anxiety will try to avoid places where there are other adults or children in order not to feel any embarrassment or discomfort. This avoidance can result in them being quite isolated from their peers and leads to them missing out on experiences. Socially anxious children often, but not always, lack social skills (i.e. they do not know how to interact with others) and this may be made worse by their lack of contact with other children and adults. Children with social anxiety are generally less anxious when they are with people they know very well, for example at home or with relatives or close friends.

Peter is a 12–year-old who experiences marked social anxiety. He hates going to school and every day he tries to get out of it, even though his mum insists that he goes. He does sometimes miss school, as his mum can't tell whether he is actually ill or not and he has on occasion vomited before school. He has two friends but does not see them out of school. Peter is described by teachers as very quiet. He prefers to stay at home or play with his cousin. He hates going to parties. At home, Peter is chatty but will not answer the telephone and is quiet if his mum and stepdad's friends come round. Peter's mum and stepdad are worried that he is too isolated and would like him to go out with friends more. They are also concerned about his school attendance and are finding the battle to get him to school every day exhausting.

In Part Two, the guide, we will discuss ways in which you can help your child to tackle some of the problems that children with shyness and social anxiety face. Our techniques can also be used with children whose shyness is less severe and is not a problem at the moment, as a way of preventing future problems from occurring. They are life skills that will stand your child in good stead for a range of problems that they might be faced with in the future.

Emily is 15 years old. She has always been shy. Emily is quiet at school and with her friends, but does socialize and mix with other teenagers. Emily hates doing PE and always tries to get her mum to write her a sick note. She is quiet around her parents' friends and is reluctant to ask for help in shops or to talk to adults she doesn't know. She tries to get her mum to pay for things when they are shopping, as she is scared she will make a mistake and be laughed at. Emily dislikes eating in front of other people as she feels self-conscious. Emily says she is happy with how things are and is just a 'home bird'. However, her parents think she is missing out on teenage activities and they worry how she will cope at university or when she gets a job.

2

Shyness and social anxiety: Thoughts, physical symptoms and behavior

The different aspects of shyness and social anxiety

Social anxiety involves an expectation that something bad is going to happen (anxious thoughts), a particular way in which our bodies respond to this (physical symptoms), and certain characteristic behaviors (anxious behavior).

Anxious thoughts

All children with anxiety have anxious thoughts and these tend to be about two things:

1 Thinking that something bad is going to happen, e.g. they will embarrass themselves, people will laugh at them or think they are stupid.

2 Thinking that they will not be able to cope with the situation, e.g. they will get upset, be sick or panic.

Children with shyness or social anxiety experience anxious thoughts about social situations; that is, they worry about what might happen in a particular social situation.

11

Shy and socially anxious children tend to fear that they will do something stupid or embarrassing in front of other people, whether adults or children, who will then judge them in a negative way. They often worry before social events that they will not cope very well, which will cause them further embarrassment.

Below are some examples of anxious thoughts that Lauren has.

> *Lauren hates answering questions in class and taking tests. Lauren has lots of anxious thoughts. She thinks that 'The children will make fun of me if I put my hand up and get a question wrong, and the teachers will tell me off and think I am stupid for being no good at my work and doing badly in my tests.' Lauren is also worried that 'If people do make fun of me, I will cry and that will be even more embarrassing.'*

Physical symptoms

We all experience physical symptoms when we are anxious, and do so because the body is preparing to deal with the perceived danger by either fighting it head-on or running away. In order to be ready to respond by fighting or fleeing, our bodies need extra energy. For instance, in the example of crossing the road and seeing a car coming, we need to get out of the way quickly. These physical symptoms are generally rather unpleasant and can be quite scary in their own right, particularly if we do not realize what they are. This is often the case for children who may not understand that these symptoms are linked to feeling scared or worried.

Although not all shy or socially anxious children experience them, common physical symptoms include choking, shaking, headaches and palpitations. Other common physical signs of anxiety are butterflies in the stomach, sweating and feeling sick or dizzy. You can see below the bodily changes that Peter experiences when he is in social situations.

> *Peter finds going to school very difficult. He often complains of stomach aches before school and his mum can see that he is breathing quickly. He also says that he feels sick and has on occasion vomited. He complains of having sweaty hands and feels his heart beating quickly. Peter gets upset by these bodily changes as they can be really uncomfortable and he worries that other children will notice them too.*

Anxious behavior

When your child is anxious, they are likely to behave in certain ways. Shy and socially anxious children tend to be quiet and withdrawn or to freeze when they are anxious. Some will also cry. They may stutter, avoid eye contact or mumble. As we have already mentioned, children with social anxiety commonly avoid a variety of situations that make them feel anxious. Occasionally, a child with social anxiety may be aggressive when they are anxious, for example hitting out or throwing things. However, this is relatively rare as the fear of what other people will think usually stops them from doing so. On the next page you can see how Michael behaved when he went to Beavers.

Michael gets very nervous about going to Beavers. On the one occasion he did attend, he froze when he arrived and did not say anything to the other children or adults. He avoided eye contact by looking down and, at one point, started to cry. Eventually, he did manage to answer the club leader's questions, but stuttered when he did so. He is still enrolled at Beavers but his mum has noticed that he seems wound up from the moment he wakes up on that day of the week. When the time approaches, he gets tearful and refuses to go. Once his parents have agreed that he doesn't have to go, he is like a different child.

We will talk more about these aspects of shyness and social anxiety later in this part when we discuss what stops your child's shyness or social anxiety from going away. In Part Two, the guide, where we outline strategies for you to use to help your child to overcome their shyness or social anxiety, we will talk in more detail about how you can help your child to change both their anxious thoughts and behavior. We do not directly address your child's physical symptoms in the main part of the book, as we and other researchers have found that if a child can change their thoughts and behaviors these physical symptoms will almost invariably disappear. However, if your child is very distressed by these bodily symptoms or they prevent your child from having a go at doing things that frighten them (one of the strategies we outline in the guide), then you may find Chapter 19, 'Relaxation', in Part Three especially helpful.

3

Is my child's shyness or social anxiety a problem?

We are guessing that, given you are continuing to read this book, you are pretty convinced that your child is shy or socially anxious. It is now important to decide whether your child's shyness or social anxiety is causing them a problem. As we said before, shyness can be viewed as a positive aspect of a child's personality. However, there are many instances when it becomes a burden and leads to children missing out on important experiences. In order to understand your child's shyness or social anxiety better, you may wish to look at the following guidelines, which we, as clinical psychologists, use to establish whether shyness or social anxiety is causing a significant problem.

The table overleaf contains a list of common social situations that many children find anxiety-provoking. Have a look and see if your child gets anxious in any of these situations. You may have to ask your child about some of these, particularly the school situations, as you may not know the answer. If your child is a teenager, they may prefer to complete the table for themselves. For the situations that do make your child anxious, try to decide how anxious they get by using the rating scale at the bottom of the table overleaf. Next, you need to think about whether your child avoids any of these situations. This means that they try their hardest not to be in this situation, or that when they are they get very upset.

Does my child experience social anxiety?		
Feared situation	**How anxious does my child feel in this situation?**	**Does my child consistently avoid this situation?**
Answering questions in class		
Asking for help in class		
Reading aloud in class		
Taking tests		
Playing with other children		
Eating in front of others		
Doing PE		
Using school toilets		
Talking on the telephone		
Attending after-school clubs		
Participating in a school play or sports day		
Talking to adults		
Talking to unfamiliar adults or children		
Going to parties		

```
0————————2————————4————————6————————8
Not at all   A little bit   Some   A lot   Very, very
                                            much
```

Now you should be able to see how many social situations your child is fearful of, how anxious they are about each situation, and whether they are currently avoiding any of them. This information should help you to decide whether your child's shyness or social anxiety is currently causing them a problem. If your child experiences a high level of anxiety in any of these situations (i.e. a rating of 4 or above), and is avoiding one or more of the social situations listed in the table whenever possible or expresses a lot of distress when in the situation, it is likely that their social anxiety is a problem.

What effect does shyness or social anxiety have on my child's life?

Social life and social skills

Shyness and social anxiety can have an enormous impact on a child's social life. During childhood, children develop friendships which enable them to learn the skills they need to interact with others and which help them to develop confidence and feel good about themselves. Having friends also gives children opportunities for having fun and learning about and from others. Children with shyness or social anxiety find interacting with their classmates very difficult and many shy and socially anxious children will avoid mixing with other children. This limits their opportunity for making friends. Some shy and socially anxious children will have good friends but may find mixing with less familiar children difficult and this will have an impact on their ability to develop the skills needed to get on with other people; indeed, many children with social anxiety do have poor social skills. In Part Two, Additional Principles 1, we talk more specifically about how you can help your child to improve their social skills.

Achieving at school

Studies suggest that children with anxiety do not do as well academically as children who do not experience significant anxiety. This is not because they are any less bright but because of problems caused by their anxiety. For example, some shy and socially anxious children find it hard to ask for help, and some may have problems concentrating due to their physical symptoms of anxiety. Both these problems may lead to them struggling with their work. Children with social anxiety sometimes miss school because they feel so nervous about the social situations that they will encounter there, such as having to answer a question in class or talk to other children or teachers. You may have noticed that your child is reluctant to attend school on occasion or even that they sometimes refuse to go (Chapter 17, 'My child won't go to school', in Part Three, discusses this in more detail). For some children, therefore, shyness or social anxiety has a major impact on their lives as it restricts their ability to fulfil their potential at school.

Mood

One in ten children with social anxiety experience symptoms of depression. These include low mood, a loss of interest in their usual activities, tearfulness or irritability, feelings of worthlessness, poor appetite and sleep problems. All children feel down from time to time, but if these symptoms persist for two weeks or more, and it seems impossible to lift your child out of their low mood, then they may be depressed. The strategies described in Part Two are useful for lots of problems and can be helpful for overcoming mild to moderate levels of depression. In this case, you may find that by helping your child to overcome their shyness and social anxiety they begin to feel better about themselves and more able to participate in activities that they will find fulfilling. However, if your child is so depressed that they are extremely withdrawn and lacking in motivation, you may find it difficult to apply many of these strategies. In this case, we would recommend that you visit your general practitioner to discuss ways in which you and your child could access additional help to improve their mood before embarking on this program.

Other anxieties

A third of children with social anxiety experience another type of anxiety problem, the most common being separation anxiety and generalized anxiety. Children with separation anxiety are fearful of being away from their parents and have difficulties with situations such as going to school, going to friends' houses or even going to bed. Children with generalized anxiety have excessive worry about lots of different things, which may include getting into trouble or academic performance, issues concerning their family or minor matters (e.g. saying the wrong thing to someone). You may have noticed that your child experiences other types of anxiety such as these. They will, of course, have a further impact on your child's life, over and above that of their social anxiety (for advice on how to help your child overcome other types of anxiety see 'Useful books and contacts').

Will my child grow out of their shyness or social anxiety?

While you may have concluded that your child's shyness or social anxiety is having a big impact on their life in the ways we have outlined above, you may well be hoping that they will grow out of it; and you may, understandably, therefore think that there is no need to do anything about it. After all, a lot of young children are shy and many of them seem to become more socially confident as they get older. To some extent, you would be right. Lots of shy children do develop into confident sociable adults. On the other hand, many shy and socially anxious children continue to be shy and socially anxious into adulthood. We talked earlier about the number of social situations that children encounter as they start school, which increase as they move on to secondary school. Some shy and socially anxious children find these situations hard to cope with and so their shyness and social anxiety become a bigger problem for them.

How can you tell whether your child will grow out of their shyness/social anxiety or not? Studies have found that children who experience high levels of social anxiety at a younger age are more likely to remain socially anxious than those whose shyness or social anxiety does not become apparent until adolescence. Although this may be worrying for you, it should not be because there is good evidence that if young children with shyness or social anxiety receive the right sort of help they are very likely to overcome their difficulties. The guide in Part Two will equip you and your child with the strategies that will enable them to do just that.

How common are shyness and social anxiety?

Having established that your child's shyness or social anxiety is having a major impact on their and possibly your family's life, it would be easy to feel that your child is the only one with such a problem. However, be reassured that this is not the case. Studies have found that between 1 in 10 and 1 in 20 children are thought to be very shy, while a smaller number, between 1 in 15 and 1 in 100, are likely to experience social anxiety that interferes significantly with their everyday life.

Certainly, social anxiety problems are not always obvious. Children with behavior difficulties, for example, often stick out due to their bad behavior and so it is clear that there is a problem. Occasionally, you may notice that a child is anxious, for instance, if they scream and run away when they see a spider. But for many anxiety disorders the signs are very subtle, and this is particularly true for shyness and social anxiety. You may notice that your child is quieter than some other children in their class, but otherwise their shyness or social anxiety is not at all obvious.

Shyness is often apparent from a young age, but it may become more evident in primary school, where children are faced with a variety of social situations, such as taking tests, answering questions and going to parties, and, even more so, in secondary school, where there is a greater need to mix with other people, both children and adults. Shyness and social anxiety are equally common in boys and girls, although shyness may be more noticeable in boys, as we have said, in whom it is seen as less socially acceptable, since boys 'should be lively and boisterous not shy and retiring'!

Is this guide appropriate for my child?

Reading the introductory chapters may have confirmed your own suspicions; that is, you may have come to the conclusion that your child is shy or socially anxious. As we have discussed, for many children shyness and social anxiety significantly interfere with their life, in that they prevent them from engaging in some social activities, such as going to clubs or parties, they make them miss out on experiences, and they may lead to different problems such as depression, other anxiety problems or difficulties in coping at school. If this is true for your child, their shyness or social anxiety warrants some intervention. The guide in this book has been designed to help you to help your child to overcome their shyness and social anxiety with a series of strategies. It includes descriptions of five children to whom you have already been introduced who have all experienced shyness or social anxiety.

Before reading about these strategies, we encourage you to read the next two chapters, where we outline some possible causes of shyness and social anxiety and some factors that might keep these problems going. A good understanding of why your child is shy or socially anxious, and, more importantly, of what is maintaining their shyness or social anxiety, will help you to put into practice more effectively the techniques we describe.

4

How do shyness and social anxiety develop in children?

Parents of anxious children who come to our clinic are almost always keen to get a better understanding of why their child is shy and socially anxious. This is partly because they want to help their child to overcome their difficulties, but sometimes it is also because they are worried that they are to blame for their child's shyness or social anxiety. It is important to stress that, although parents can influence their child's shyness or social anxiety, such problems rarely result from only one source. They are likely to be the outcome of a variety of factors or influences. We will talk about the most important factors in this chapter: what children inherit from their family; what they learn from others around them; and the effect that adverse life events, such as bereavements, might have.

What do we inherit?

We all inherit certain physical characteristics from our parents, such as the colour of our hair, our facial mannerisms or our stature. The same is true for psychological traits. It appears that genes do play a role in the transmission from one generation to the next of particular psychological problems such as some types of depression or behaviors (such as having a short temper or being overactive).

The same pattern can be seen with anxiety. Studies have found that anxiety runs in families, which suggests that anxiety may be passed on genetically from one generation to another. However, anxiety may also be transmitted by individuals' behavior influencing that of others in the family. Studies suggest that about one-third of the influence on whether or not we are anxious is caused by genetics. In other words, anxiety is caused by one part genes and two parts environment (i.e. what we learn from those around us and our experiences).

The same appears to be true specifically for shyness and social anxiety. Studies have found that shyness and social anxiety run in families and that they are partly inherited but that they may also be influenced by what children learn from others around them. Studies have also found that where a family member experiences social anxiety, other family members may be more likely to experience one or more of a variety of anxiety problems. So, for example, if your child is shy or socially anxious, you may have noticed that other members of your family may be shy or socially anxious too, or that they may experience a different type of anxiety, such as excessive worrying or a specific fear (e.g. phobia of dogs).

Not only is a tendency to become anxious likely to be inherited, but we can also inherit certain personality traits; and some types of personality traits make us more likely to develop anxiety. You may hear other parents sometimes say, 'He has always been like this,' or 'He was born like it.' What they are referring to is one aspect of their child's personality or temperament that they noticed at a young age. Studies have found that children who, as babies and toddlers, were fearful of new situations, people or events, such as going to a mother and toddler group for the first time or going to see a health visitor or doctor, and who became distressed if they had to mix with unfamiliar adults or children, were more likely to develop social anxiety when they got older. From the example below, you will see that Michael's mum noticed that Michael had this type of temperament when he was very young.

When Michael was a toddler, his mum took him to a toddler coffee morning. Michael got very upset and clung to his mother for the whole session. He didn't mix with the other children or talk to the other mums. He didn't like playing with the noisy toys. Although some of the other children at these groups were a bit shy and took a little while to settle in, Michael's behavior was more marked. Michael's mum gave up taking him after just a few sessions because it was so stressful for both of them. She also noticed that Michael got upset when she took him into any new situation, such as swimming or to a new play area.

Although a child's genetic make-up is important in the development of shyness and social anxiety, it is also important to remember that not all children who inherit a tendency to shyness or anxiety become shy or anxious. There are many children who have a shy or anxious parent, grandparent or sibling, but who are not shy or socially anxious themselves. Similarly, there are lots of children who found new situations difficult as young children, but who are now socially confident and outgoing.

What do we learn from those around us?

So far we have talked about the role of your child's genetic make-up in making them more vulnerable to being shy or developing social anxiety. This is obviously something that is beyond your control! However, do not despair, as this is not the whole story. Genes play only a small part in the development of anxiety. What a child learns from their environment is crucially important. Children observe and copy other people, and they notice how other people respond to them in tricky situations, particularly people to whom they are close or whom they regard highly. These factors will have an influence on whether your child becomes shy or develops social anxiety or not and can, of course, be changed both by you as parents and other people around your child.

Picking up on anxious behavior

From a young age, one way in which children learn is by observing and copying others. Children are more likely to copy the behavior of people they are close to and with whom they have most contact. This invariably means you, their main carer(s), and other important family members, such as siblings. Children copy helpful behavior from you and others around them, but they may learn unhelpful ways of behaving too.

Lauren's mum sympathizes with her daughter as she also finds some social situations a bit nerve-racking, although she tries to hide this from Lauren. Lauren's mum likes to keep herself to herself and doesn't often go out to socialize. A close friend has asked her to join a yoga class but she is not keen to go as she worries that she might make a fool of herself. Lauren's mum works in quite a sociable office but she tries to avoid going out after work if she can. Lauren's mum also finds mixing with other parents at Lauren's school hard; for example when she drops Lauren off at school each morning or when she attends a school play or parents' evening. She often says to her daughter that she doesn't fancy going, although she doesn't tell her why.

As a parent, if you behave in an anxious way your child is likely to sense this. Most parents try to conceal their anxious behavior for this very reason, but children are extremely good at picking up on subtle cues and are likely to know that something is wrong.

Responding to your child in difficult situations

How people respond to your child when they are faced with difficult situations is important and can influence how well your child learns to cope when they are nervous. Children need to experience a certain amount of anxiety so that they learn how to deal with it. Remember how Michael became distressed as a toddler in new or unfamiliar situations. His distress was hard for his mum to deal with so eventually she stopped taking him to places that made him feel anxious. Unfortunately, by doing so she did not allow Michael the opportunity to tolerate some anxiety and to learn how to cope with it and overcome it. Michael's mum was simply trying to protect him from any upset, as we all instinctively try to do as parents. However, although Michael was bound to feel better in the short term, in the longer term it did not help him to develop the skills necessary to deal with other tricky situations when they arose.

> Peter's mother and stepfather used to try to get him to go to parties but now can't bring themselves to do it as Peter gets so upset and they do not like to see him in such a state. Peter often comes home upset from school because a child has teased him or would not let him hang around with him. Peter's mum then goes into school straight away to see the teacher as she knows Peter will worry about it a lot and will have trouble sleeping so she thinks it is best to get it sorted out.

Parents often try to sort out problems for their child, as Peter's mum does in the example above. A child may come home upset, for instance, and say they have fallen out with another child. In an attempt to make your child feel better, you might go into school to try to solve the problem, perhaps by talking to the teacher or possibly the parent of the other child. However, in sorting out your child's problems for them, you are not allowing them to practise ways to deal with them themselves and you are also unintentionally giving them the message that you do not think they can solve the problem for themselves. Only by trying to sort out their own problems, with your help and support, will your child be able to develop their own problem-solving skills, in addition to feeling less anxious and more confident.

Adverse life events

Peter's mother and father separated when he was 6 years old. At the same time, Peter and his mum moved house and so Peter had to change schools. His mum reports that he found all these changes very hard and that she really noticed his social anxiety around this time. She wonders whether these events caused Peter to become anxious.

We all experience significant events at some point in our lives. These may include the death of a family member or close friend, the birth of a sibling, moving house, school or job, or illness in the family. It is a common belief that it is these types of life events that lead children, or indeed adults, to become anxious. As you can see from the example above, Peter's mum couldn't help wondering if this had caused his social anxiety. However, it is not clear whether these events actually cause anxiety or whether children and adults who are already anxious simply find such events harder to deal with and as a result become even more anxious. Certainly, an adverse life event on its own is not enough to cause a child to become anxious. You can probably think of other children you know who have had to contend with difficult circumstances, but have responded to this in quite different ways. Other factors, such as your child's genetic make-up or what they have learned from those around them, will also contribute.

What has made my child anxious?

As we have outlined, your child's shyness or social anxiety is likely to have been caused by several factors, including their genetic make-up, what they have learned from others around them, and possibly any major negative events that they have experienced. The relative importance of these factors will be different for each child. You cannot, of course, change your child's genetic make-up or indeed most of the life events that they experience. However, you can have a great deal of influence on what your child learns from those around them and we will be talking more about what you can do to influence your child's environment in Step 3 of Part Two. At this point, it is important to emphasize that it is vital to focus on what is keeping your child's problems going, as this is what needs to change in order to help them to overcome their shyness or social anxiety. The next chapter explores what these factors might be.

5

What stops my child's shyness or social anxiety from going away?

Vicious cycles

In Chapter 2, we described the three components of shyness and social anxiety: anxious thoughts; physical symptoms; and anxious behavior. These three parts of shyness and social anxiety work together to maintain your child's anxiety, as you can see from Peter's example below.

Peter
Social situation: Going to a party

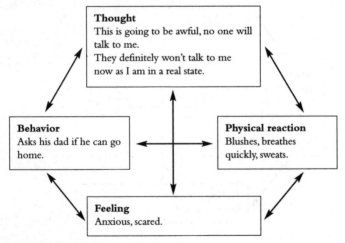

Thought
This is going to be awful, no one will talk to me.
They definitely won't talk to me now as I am in a real state.

Behavior
Asks his dad if he can go home.

Physical reaction
Blushes, breathes quickly, sweats.

Feeling
Anxious, scared.

What stops my child's shyness or social anxiety from going away?

When Peter goes to a party, he thinks, 'This is going to be awful, no one will talk to me.' He starts blushing, breathing quickly and sweating. Now Peter is thinking, 'They definitely won't talk to me now as they can see I am in a real state.' This convinces Peter that it really is going to be a bad experience so he tries to get away. He says to his dad, 'I can't stay, I'm too scared, can I go home?' His dad agrees and Peter feels better. He thinks, 'Thank goodness I went home before I made a fool of myself.' The next time Peter is invited to a party he decides not to go, as he feels sure that he will have a bad time.

The diagrams below and overleaf show similar vicious cycles that Michael and Lauren experience.

Michael
Social situation: Joining in a game at playtime

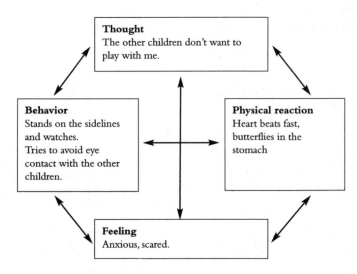

Lauren

Social situation: Having a test at school

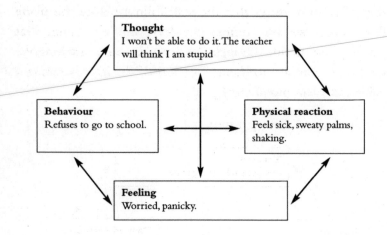

Anxious thinking

We talked in Chapter 2 about how children with shyness or social anxiety have two common types of thought: they *overestimate* how likely it is that something bad is going to happen; they *underestimate* their ability to cope with what may happen. People with anxiety are on the lookout for things that back up their anxious thoughts. For example, someone who is scared of flying is likely to listen out for odd noises, look for rust or holes on the side of the plane, or anything unusual when they get on a plane! Someone who is scared of making a speech will look at their audience when they are speaking to see if anyone is laughing or frowning, to back up their thoughts that they are doing a bad job. They won't notice the people who are listening intently, nodding or even smiling to show their approval. Similarly, the person who is scared of flying won't notice that perhaps it is a brand-new plane or will disregard all the safety procedures that the staff follow before the plane flies. When we are anxious, we look out for things that confirm our anxious thoughts and we discount anything we see that is contrary to them. This way of thinking becomes a habit and keeps our anxiety going.

Social situation: Giving a speech

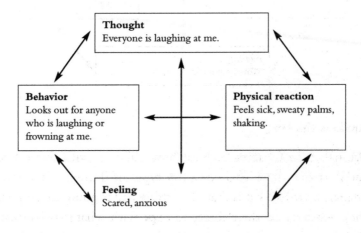

Physical symptoms

Physical symptoms of anxiety can make your child's shyness or social anxiety worse. Remember Peter's example. When he blushed, began to sweat and breathe faster, he predicted that the situation would get worse as no one would talk to him when he was in such a state. So Peter's physical symptoms of anxiety actually made him believe his anxious thoughts even more. Similarly, when Lauren started to shake before taking a test, she was worried that she would not be able to write properly. Her physical symptoms made her anxiety worse.

Lauren
Social situation: Having a test at school

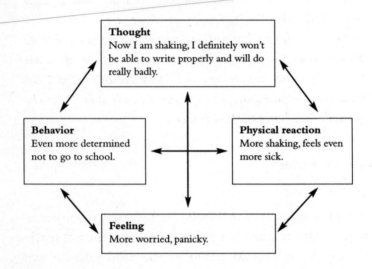

Physical symptoms, associated with social anxiety and shyness, can be quite confusing for children. It is hard for them to understand that worry or anxiety can actually cause a pain in their body. This is particularly true for symptoms such as stomach aches or headaches which children get for lots of different reasons. These symptoms are often a problem for parents too, who are understandably not sure whether the pain is due to anxiety or a medical problem of some sort. To be on the safe side, parents will often allow their child to miss school when they have this sort of physical symptom, but they are inadvertently allowing their child to avoid the very thing that makes them anxious. Below is an example of the dilemma many parents find themselves in.

> *Lauren often complains of headaches before school and gets upset when her mum sends her anyway. Lauren's mum is never sure whether she should send her to school or not, but does so now as she thinks Lauren's headaches are probably due to anxiety. Lauren cries when her mum sends her and her mum feels really guilty but she knows it is for the best. School has promised to send Lauren home if she is clearly unwell but she generally feels better once she is there.*

Anxious behavior

Avoidance

A common reaction when faced with threat or danger is to run away. This is sensible behavior if the situation is dangerous. For example, getting out of the road when a car is coming is clearly a good idea! However, children who are shy or socially anxious see threat in social situations when it may not actually exist. As we have said, they overestimate the chances of something bad happening and as a result avoid social situations if they can, for example refusing to go to school or trying to get out of doing PE. The problem with avoiding situations is that your child will never learn that nothing bad did happen or that they did cope okay in the situation. Overleaf is an example of how Peter's avoidance of parties has made his anxiety worse.

Peter really dislikes going to parties as they make him feel very nervous. He worries about having to talk to children he doesn't know very well. Peter used to go to parties when he was younger, but in the past two years he has started avoiding them. Since Peter has stopped going to parties, his fear of them has actually got much worse and he can't ever see himself going again. He can't imagine how he would cope at a party now and has no idea what he might say to children whom he doesn't really know. At least when he was going to parties, Peter could think about how he coped at the last one and it wasn't usually as bad as he thought it was going to be. However, now, the longer he avoids going to parties, the worse his fear gets as it is harder to remember that sometimes he did have a pretty good time.

Safety behaviors

Children with shyness or social anxiety also try to avoid anxiety in more subtle ways. When they are in a social situation that makes them feel anxious, they do things in a certain way or have items with them that help them to feel safe. Here are some examples of safety behaviors that shy or socially anxious children may engage in:

- Always having someone with them for support i.e. Mum being there;
- Taking a special toy with them; carrying a bottle of water so they can sip it if they feel nervous;
- Wearing a hood or growing their hair long so people can't see them very well.

Although these behaviors help children to feel better, they are actually preventing them from facing their fears, and afterwards they will commonly believe that they were only able to cope because they had the bottle of water, Mum was there and so on. Eventually, children need to learn that they can manage in social situations without these props.

Your child's environment

Reassurance

All parents reassure their children and, in the short term, it makes our children feel better. Children with shyness or social anxiety seek a lot of reassurance and they too initially feel better when they receive it. However, you have probably noticed that the reassurance you give your child doesn't seem to last for long and that they come back again and again for more. In the longer term, reassurance does not help your child to develop the confidence that they can deal with the problem. In fact, reassurance ensures that they will go on needing you to tell them that it will be okay, when instead they need to learn for themselves that they can cope. Giving lots of reassurance unfortunately leads to your child becoming more dependent on you. In contrast, in this book our aim is to help your child have the skills and confidence to be independent. We will talk in Steps 2 and 3 about how you can replace reassurance with other, more helpful responses.

Other unhelpful responses

We have already talked in Chapter 4 about how other people might respond to your child or how your child might notice other people's anxious behavior. These factors also help to maintain your child's anxiety and become part of a vicious cycle. If people around your child show signs of anxiety and avoid situations that make them anxious, your child (who will be on the lookout for information that confirms their anxious thoughts) is likely to learn that the particular situation presents a threat and the best way to respond is by avoiding it. Equally, if those close to your child allow them to avoid social situations, this will also give them the message that there is something to fear or that they will be unable to cope. Once again, your child is now more likely to try to avoid these situations. Finally, if your child does not get the opportunities to experience social situations, despite their shyness or social anxiety, they will not learn that in fact the situation was not as bad as they thought it would be and that they managed to cope. Your child will also have limited opportunities to develop good social skills, which, in themselves, will give them more confidence about interacting with others.

What can I do to break these cycles?

The main aim of the five steps of the guide is to help you and your child to break the negative cycles that are keeping their shyness or social anxiety going. The strategies that we describe will help your child to think in a less anxious way and will help them to have a go at doing things, particularly social activities, rather than avoiding doing them as they are almost certainly doing at the moment. You, as a parent or carer, will have a crucial role to play. You will need to motivate your child, develop a good understanding of the strategies that we present to you, so that you can share them with your child, and be aware of your own behavior and how it affects your child. We acknowledge that what we are asking you to do is not easy, but, having seen how successful parents and carers can be at helping their child to overcome their difficulties, we are confident that you too can rise to the challenge.

PART TWO

Overcoming Your Child's Shyness or Social Anxiety

6

Introduction to the guide

Many children experience difficulties with shyness or social anxiety, and often families are able to overcome these problems without professional support. For some children, their shyness or social anxiety seems just to be a phase that they grow out of. For others, their shyness or social anxiety may exist without causing any particular problems for them or their family. They are not avoiding anything and they are not bothered by the presence of their anxiety (e.g. a child who is fearful of performing in a school play but very rarely actually has to do so). For some others, however, their shyness or social fears are more persistent or cause more disruption to their own or their families' lives. You may have noticed that your child frequently becomes distressed and may be avoiding certain activities because of their shyness or social anxiety. You and other members of your family may be working so hard to minimize your child's distress that coping becomes very stressful and time-consuming, or your family ends up avoiding social activities that you enjoy because they upset your child so much. For some families, specialist help is required, and it is important that they seek this help and receive it. Many families could, however, if they knew how, overcome these difficulties themselves.

This book is designed to help families who are prepared to have a go at helping their child to overcome their shyness and social anxiety but who are unsure where to begin. We take you through a series of steps which introduce you to a range of strategies to help to overcome your child's problem. Although this book is intended to help families whose child's shyness or social anxiety is causing a significant problem, as we have described before, the strategies can also be used with children who are only experiencing minor difficulties. The techniques we describe in the guide are life skills that can be used by any child, with the help of their parent(s), to learn to cope with a variety of social situations that they may encounter. Developing these skills will help to prevent future problems and will lead to your child becoming a more confident and sociable individual.

Using this guide with children of different ages

The strategies outlined in the guide can be used with children of all ages. However, the emphasis is on techniques appropriate for 8–11-year-olds, and therefore the techniques do need some adaptation for use with younger children and with teenagers. For each step of the guide, we will outline the strategies that you can use with your child, using examples to highlight some of these techniques. If your child is older than 11 or younger than 8, you may well need to fine-tune some of the strategies by using the tips and hints that we provide throughout the guide. There are also some general principles to bear in mind when working with a teenager, which we have outlined in the next section of the book. If you are a parent of a teenager, we urge you to read this brief section before moving on to the guide itself.

7

Using this guide with teenagers

If you have a teenager who is shy or socially anxious, there are factors that may make your job of helping them especially difficult. It is important to be aware of these before embarking on using this guide so that you can be prepared to overcome them. Teenagers are more likely to be reluctant to co-operate and may think that you are simply interfering. Teenagers are also likely to be particularly sensitive to what they imagine other people are thinking about them. One of the biggest challenges you will face is talking to your teenager in a way that lets them feel that you are genuinely interested in their point of view, that you are not criticizing or making fun of them but taking them seriously. If you can successfully show your teenager that you are willing to listen and try to understand their shyness or social anxiety problems, then you are well on your way to helping them to overcome them. For your teenager to work with you, you need to show that you accept what they are worried about and that you are not judging them. However, it is essential that you recognize that their shyness or social anxiety is getting in the way and something needs to be done about it.

Does your teenager want to change?

Although you may view your teenager's shyness or social

anxiety as being problematic, it is possible that they do not feel the same way. If this is the case, many of the strategies described in the guide will be difficult to use. The main focus should be on the way in which you respond to your teenager (Step 3 of the guide). Nonetheless, we would still encourage you to read the other steps of the guide as you will be able to use these techniques to some degree, such as trying not to reinforce avoidance (Step 4), praising and rewarding any efforts your teenager makes to face their fears (Step 4), responding to your teenager's fears with helpful questions rather than reassurance (Steps 1 and 2), and encouraging your teenager to solve problems for themselves (Step 5). In order to use the techniques in many of the steps fully, however, you will need to wait until your teenager is ready to work with you. Telling your child that they *have* to do the things in this book will lead to more reluctance on their part. Instead, ask about their goals and whether their shyness or social anxiety will create any difficulties in achieving these goals. In the end, the choice is your child's, but your job is to help them to make an *informed* choice. Here's an example of a conversation between Emily and her dad:

Father:	*Emily, I saw this book and thought you might like it. It's about trying to be more confident and less shy.*
Emily:	*There is nothing wrong with being shy.*
Father:	*I agree, but sometimes your shyness gets in the way a bit, don't you think?*

Emily: Not really.

Father: Not at all?

Emily: Maybe, the odd time.

Father: When are you thinking of?

Emily: I don't know. Maybe when I wanted to go on holiday with Lucy but I felt a bit awkward about talking to her parents and eating in front of them. I don't like PE as you well know but I am hardly missing out!

Father: Yes, it must have been a bit tricky on that holiday. I can see you're not too worried about PE though. What about eating at school?

Emily: I'm not sure that is a problem, I just don't eat.

Father: Yes, I know, but it might get in the way in the future and you would miss out, that's all I was thinking.

Emily: I'm more likely to miss out because I don't like talking to adults than not wanting to eat in front of my friends. I can just not eat.

Father: I see your point. What about university?

Emily: What about it?

Father: Do you think being shy will cause any problems there?

Emily: I don't know. It might be a bit hard.

Father: I think you are probably right. It could be pretty tough.

Emily: Yeah, maybe, but I don't know if I can change. I am just shy.

Father: *Well, why don't you read this? If you'd like your mum and me to give this a try with you, we'd really like to.*

Giving teenagers more control

The main difference in helping teenagers as opposed to children to overcome their shyness or social anxiety is that teenagers need to be put in a position of greater control over the strategies they use. Although your teenage child still needs your support and guidance, they will be more equipped to carry out some of the strategies independently and, in fact, are likely to want to do them independently, rather than have you tell them what to do (we have included separate records sheets for teenagers in Appendix 6 for this reason)! It is really important to remember this. If you insist on taking charge, your teenager is likely to lose interest and refuse to participate at all. A good starting point might be to get your teenager to read this book so that they can decide whether they think it is worth a try. By doing this, you are immediately giving them more control, rather than telling them what to do. Then, perhaps you can ask them which strategy they want to work on first, which makes most sense to them, and how they would like you to help. In this way, you are allowing them to take the lead. It is also worth asking who else they think might be able to help them have a go at some of the tasks in this book. Are there friends or other adults who could give them a bit of support? Although as parents you will want to help, sometimes your teenager will find it easier to accept help from others rather than from you.

Hopefully, your teenager will decide that it is worth reading this book. If they do, it is still important for you to read it too, as it is essentially a book for parents, and it provides you with the tools you will need to support and guide your teenager in overcoming their shyness or social anxiety.

8

How to use this guide

Why change?

It would be understandable if, at this point, you had some mixed feelings about changing things in your child's, and your own, life. Looking after a child who is shy or socially anxious can be anxiety-provoking in itself, and often quite tiring, and it is likely that it has taken a great effort on your part to get by as well as you have and to have kept your child's distress to a minimum. We are sure that you will think that, inevitably, this program is going to involve your child facing up to their anxiety about social situations. You have probably tried this before and may well have found that this caused more upset than seemed worthwhile. Maybe, you think, you should just carry on as you are. Perhaps you think that they'll grow out of it. Maybe you are worried that trying to do something now will just make matters worse. These are all understandable reactions to the prospect of changing things. Our hunch is that if you are reading this book then you must think that you have reached the point where your child's shyness or social anxiety is getting in the way to some extent. There is good research to show that children are likely to be successful in overcoming their shyness or social anxiety if the principles in this book are used consistently and regularly. Applying these principles may not always be easy; in fact it is prudent to prepare yourself for the fact that there will be obstacles and setbacks along the way. Sometimes, too, things can seem to get worse before they get better simply because by taking action you are changing the status quo. You need to be aware of this in order to pick the right moment to embark on the program.

When to change?

It is worth considering whether now is the best time to be working with your child on overcoming their shyness or social anxiety. In order to apply the principles in this book without fail you will need to make this your top priority for the next couple of months. If you are about to go on holiday for two weeks, or you are approaching a major deadline at work, you are not going to be able to commit yourself sufficiently to this program. Similarly, if your child is about to go away on a school trip, you don't want to make a start that can't be followed up for over a week. In these circumstances, it would be best to postpone beginning the program until you are in a position to make this your number one priority. Having said that, however, there may always seem to be one reason or another to put off making a start but, unless there is a serious reason for not starting (like those given above), you should set yourself a start date in the near future. What we would suggest is that you begin now by reading through this entire part, the guide, within the next week or so. You will then have a clear idea of what will be involved in order to set your date to get started with your child.

What to change?

While a small number of children we work with seem to experience just one very specific social fear or anxiety (e.g. taking tests), the majority of children we work with experience anxiety about a number of different social situations. If your child has just one fear then you will have no problem in deciding what to focus on. If, however, in common with most shy and socially anxious children, your child seems to worry about all sorts of social situations, you will need to decide early on which you are going to make your focus. It is very important that you choose *one* particular social fear to concentrate on (you can use the table you completed in Chapter 3 to remind you what your child's social fears are). This keeps things simpler for you and your child and gains that are made will be obvious to you both. It may be that by picking one fear you feel that you are dealing with just 'the tip of the iceberg' but this need not put you off for two reasons. First, skills will be learned and practised by you and your child. It will then be easier to apply them to other fears (one by one). Second, overcoming one fear successfully will teach your child some valuable lessons which will have knock-on effects for other fears: (a) that fears can be overcome, and (b) that they are capable of overcoming them. You may also find that many of your child's social fears overlap, so by tackling one fear, you may, in fact, be partly tackling another.

About the self-help program

The following sections provide you with the key information. We outline steps you can use to overcome your child's shyness and social anxiety. These are the basic elements of cognitive-behavior therapy for children with anxiety problems. Cognitive-behavior therapy refers to treatment based on the premise that how we think about things is associated with how we behave and how we feel. Therefore, by changing how we think about our fears and how we act because of them we can change how we feel about them. This type of therapy is widely used with adults and children and has in the last decade become the treatment of choice for many emotional problems, particularly anxiety difficulties. A number of treatment studies have shown that where the principles described in this book are followed consistently children benefit considerably.

The five steps

The five main principles of the treatment are shown in the table opposite. These principles can also be regarded as steps, as they follow each other in the order given.

In addition to the five steps shown in the table, there are two additional sections at the end of this main part. The first of these outlines how you can help to improve your child's social skills. Some children with social anxiety have been found to have particular difficulties interacting with other people. Many other socially anxious children have the necessary skills but lack confidence in their ability to interact with others. This section will help you to decide whether your child needs to learn particular social skills and gives you a guide on how to help them do so. It also shows you how to increase your child's confidence in interacting with others.

Step 1 Learning to spot your child's anxious thoughts

(Asking the right questions and listening to the answers!)

Step 2 Helping your child to evaluate their thoughts and consider other points of view

(Asking the right questions to help your child work out if their thoughts are reasonable and/or helpful. Helping your child to test out other ways of thinking about the fear.)

Step 3 Encouraging independence and having a go

(Using praise and rewards to encourage non-anxious behavior.)

Step 4 Developing a step-by-step plan with your child

(Helping your child to make a plan for gradually facing their fears.)

Step 5 Problem-solving

(Asking the right questions to help your child become an independent problem-solver.)

The second of these sections concerns managing your own anxiety. Many parents of the anxious children we see also experience difficulties with anxiety themselves. Often parents are shy or socially anxious too, and sometimes parents of shy and socially anxious children experience different types of anxiety, such as high levels of worrying. It has been found that where parents are very anxious, if their anxiety is dealt with first, then their child is more likely to benefit from treatment. This is probably because if you are less anxious not only will you find it easier to follow this program but also your child will start to learn other ways of thinking and behaving from you. If you are an anxious or shy person yourself, you may find it hard to create the right opportunities for your child to overcome their shyness or social anxiety. For example, if you get nervous about going to social gatherings and try to avoid them, your child probably seldom goes to social gatherings either and so doesn't get the opportunity to tackle their fears about social occasions. By making a concerted effort to overcome your own shyness or anxiety, you will not only be helping yourself but you will also be helping your child to become less shy or socially anxious. We would encourage you to read this chapter before you actually embark upon the five steps.

The parents' role

Throughout this program there is a big emphasis on you helping your child to overcome their shyness or social anxiety. Rather than solving problems for your child, or reassuring them that everything will be fine, your role will be to act as both coach and 'cheerleader'. You will be in charge of helping your child to work out what to do for themselves and then cheering on their progress. At the end of the day it will be your child who has to deal with problems; you cannot guarantee that you'll always be there when a problem arises, so it is essential that your child is learning, with help from you, how to deal with their shyness or social anxiety themselves. Nonetheless it is quite likely that you see your child's shyness or social anxiety as a bigger problem than they do. For example, if a child is anxious about attending school, they are unlikely to think that the answer is to overcome this fear and go to school. Instead, they will think that the best course of action is simply not to go to school. Although you need to work with and guide your child, it is also your responsibility to encourage, motivate and set a good example to them. The extent to which you take the lead will vary depending on the age of your child. Certainly for young children and primary school-aged children, we would expect you to take the lead; while with teenagers, you will need to work as a team with your teenager, encouraging and motivating them, rather than telling them what to do.

As you will have seen from the table of steps, much of your job involves asking your child questions to help them work things out for themselves (for young children, you will need to be much more proactive in helping your child to find alternative ways of thinking and behaving but the principles remain the same). To help your child do so successfully you need to ask the right questions. This is not always easy, but we will help you. It is essential that the questions are asked in a way that shows your child that you are taking their worries seriously and that you are not making fun or being critical. This can be difficult at times, particularly if you are feeling frustrated by your child's behavior. For your child to work with you, you need to show that you understand and accept what they are worried about. However, you need to communicate that you also recognize that this worry is getting in the way and so something needs to be done about it. While the worries themselves need to be taken seriously, in working together to overcome them take every opportunity to have fun and be creative. If the whole program is heavy and emotional your child is not going to want to be involved; so, particularly when it comes to Step 3 onwards, try to lighten the mood and enjoy yourselves!

Keeping written records

Throughout the book we ask you to keep records of the work you do with your child. Some parents like to work through these with their child, while others complete them alone. For parents of teenagers, we recommend that your teenager keeps the records, rather than you (see Appendix 6 for records for teenagers). There are two reasons why it is essential that you or your teenager do put pen to paper and complete the records. First, writing things down helps learning and remembering. Second, this gives you or your teenager a marker to refer back to at later times. Often parents and children will feel as if things have been moving backwards, but then when they look at their written records they see that in fact progress has been made. It is easy for what is happening right now to feel as if it has been happening forever but this is generally not the case.

You don't need to go it alone

We often work with single parents who put this program into practice very successfully on their own. There is no doubt, however, that it will be easier to work through the program with your child if you have help from others around you. This may be a partner, parent, older child, a friend, or your child's teacher. As we mentioned earlier, teenagers may also wish to be supported by another person they know well, such as a friend or teacher. The more people around your child who are following the same principles, the easier it will be for your child to learn how to overcome their social fears. Equally, working with another adult is likely to motivate you and keep you going at times when it feels like a struggle. Also, as is shown on the table, this program includes practising ways of talking to your child to help them, for example, explain what their worry is and consider other ways of thinking. Sometimes the strategies we suggest may be tricky. In particular it can be difficult to stick to asking questions, rather than giving your child reassurance or trying to solve problems for them. You may feel embarrassed at first, but having a practice run at these conversations with another adult will really help to prepare you for talking through these matters with your child. Your 'partner' can help you to decide which questions worked well, whether the tone was right and whether they felt understood and taken seriously.

Keeping it going

The final section in this part is all about keeping your child's progress going. It is likely that having read all the way through this book you will feel charged up and ready to tackle your child's difficulties. But it is just as likely that this determination will plummet when you hit your first hurdle. You may feel as if you've failed, that you're not doing it properly and that your child will never recover. It is really important to stress that if overcoming your child's problems were easy, you would have done it long ago. You must understand that there *will* be setbacks, times when your child does not make as much progress as you had hoped, or even seems to go backwards. Be reassured that this is normal. Your child has been set in a pattern of thinking, behaving and feeling in a certain way for some time, and this is not going to change overnight. However, if you follow the principles described here you will be helping your child to take control of their shyness or social anxiety and you will almost certainly make progress.

So now it is time to take your first step and read what is involved in helping your child overcome their shyness or social anxiety.

Good luck!

9

Step 1: Spotting socially anxious thinking

Note: Read through all of Step 1 before trying to put any of the strategies into effect.

Seeing danger everywhere

As we discussed earlier, children who are shy or socially anxious tend to think about things in a particular way. You may have noticed that your child tends to see danger all around them; for example attending an after-school club or youth club for the first time would cause enormous anxiety for many shy or socially anxious children. This is not surprising given that shy and socially anxious children are often worried that other children will not like them or will laugh at them. In fact, shy and socially anxious children are 'on the lookout' for threat and 'jump to conclusions' about threat, and if what is going on is not absolutely clear they will interpret it as threatening. What's more, a shy or socially anxious child will think that they are not going to be able to deal with the dangers thrown at them, and are likely to become distressed. These ways of thinking are associated with anxiety even in young children (from pre-school age) so we would recommend having a go at the tasks in this chapter with any child who can talk about their fears. If your child is young (seven years of age or younger), we will discuss ways of adapting these strategies so that they are more effective for this age group. These strategies aim to teach children to respond to fears or anxieties in a helpful way, so can also be used with non-anxious children. By doing so, you may prevent your child from developing anxiety problems in the future.

Helpful and unhelpful thoughts

Lauren had a part in the school play. In common with many children, she is anxious and thinks that she won't be able to do it or will make a mess of it. She expects that she will get really scared and won't be able to remember her lines. All the other children will laugh at her and think she is stupid, as you can see from the diagram opposite. No wonder she feels anxious! And no wonder that she will probably feel quite sick before the performance and won't want to go to school. Sarah also has a part in the school play. As you can see from the diagram opposite, she also feels a bit nervous about it but she thinks that everyone else is likely to be nervous too so the rest of the school will understand how she feels. She thinks it will probably be fine, but if not it will soon be over and forgotten about. On the day of the play, Sarah feels a little nervous but goes in and performs in the play.

From these examples we can see that, although the situation is the same, different thoughts are associated with different feelings and different actions. Some thoughts can be quite

Step 1: Spotting socially anxious thinking

Lauren:

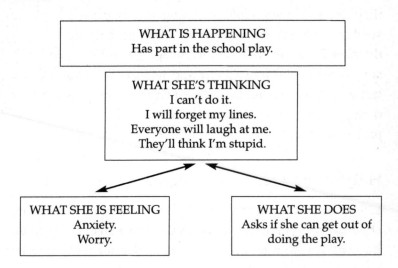

Sarah:

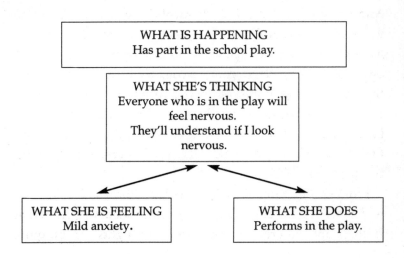

helpful; they help us to feel calm and stop us missing out on things. Other thoughts can be unhelpful; they make us more anxious and stop us having a go at things that we might enjoy or that might be good for us.

How do I know what my child is thinking?

If you are not sure what your child is thinking in a particular social situation, try asking them. This may seem like an easy task, and for some parents and children it is, but for others it can be quite tricky. One reason is that your child may not really know why they are worried. Sometimes these thoughts pop into our heads so quickly that we hardly notice them. For that reason it is useful to try to ask your child about their worries when they happen, rather than much later.

Some children find it hard to say what they are worried about as other people are present and they feel self-conscious. This is particularly true for shy and socially anxious children and even more so for shy teenagers. It may mean you cannot ask about the worries right at the time of anxiety. In this case, try to create a comfortable environment in which to talk to your child as soon as possible after the event.

Asking questions

On the next page are some examples of questions you can ask to help your child to tell you what it is that worries them. Use these questions when you spot signs that your child is feeling anxious (e.g. from their behavior, from bodily symptoms).

Spotting unhelpful thoughts

Sample questions to ask:

Why are you worried?
What is frightening you?
What do you think will happen?
What is it (about this situation) that is making you worried?

Clearly, there is nothing very clever or magical about these questions. But there are two main points to keep in mind. First, these questions all start with 'What' or 'Why'. These are called 'open' questions. Compare these to what are called 'closed' questions; for example, 'Do you worry that you will get hurt?', 'Are you worried that the other children will laugh at you?' To 'closed' questions your child can just give you a 'Yes' or 'No' answer which may not help you to get a better understanding of how they are thinking. 'Open' questions, on the other hand, do not limit the response in this way, and you are likely to get much more helpful information. We would recommend that you try to stick to 'open' questions as much as possible.

Second, think about *how* you ask these questions. Consider different ways of asking the first question. How you ask the question should give your child the message that you can see that they are worried and you want to help. In contrast, asking 'Why (on earth!) are you worried?' may make a child much more reluctant to answer as there is a clear message that they really should not be worried in this situation and are bad or silly for thinking the way they do.

Teenagers are generally good at knowing what they are worried about. However, it is still worthwhile asking your teenager what it is they find anxiety-provoking, so that they become familiar with the questions we have listed above. Once your teenager is familiar with them, they can ask them themselves at times when they are anxious or worried. It is important for your teenager to do this, as they need to be able to say what they are worried about in order to use the strategies in Step 2.

Questions to ask young children

For younger children, you need to ask simple questions, using simple language, such as, 'What do you think is going to happen?' Young children often find it easier to describe something happening to someone else rather than themselves, so, for example, it can help to use dolls or action figures to set up a story about a social situation that would frighten your child and ask what would happen to the dolls in the story. Your child may tell quite a fantastical story, but you are likely to be able to pick up useful or important themes. For example, do they think someone will laugh at them, that someone will be nasty to them, or that someone will think they are stupid?

If that doesn't work

In order to tell you about their thoughts, your child must really believe that you are asking because you want to understand their worries better in order to help them through these anxieties. It may be that the first time you ask these questions your child is reluctant to express their fears. But as you continue to ask these sorts of questions in the social situations in which your child is fearful they might find it easier to answer. If you feel you have been asking these questions for a while and in each situation you have exhausted your 'open' questions, then you may need to encourage your child by talking about what might make *you* worry in a similar social situation. For example, Peter didn't want to go to his friend's party. The following discussion went on between Peter and his father:

Dad:	*Peter, are you going to go to Adam's party on Saturday?*
Peter:	*No.*
Dad:	*What are you worried about?*
Peter:	*I just don't want to go.*
Dad:	*But why is that? What do you think will happen when you are there?*
Peter:	*I won't like it. I won't know anyone.*
Dad:	*I see. Why does that worry you?*
Peter:	*It just won't be very nice.*
Dad:	*I suppose if I had to go to a party where I didn't know anyone, I might be worried too. I might be worried that I might not like any of the boys there. Is that what you are worried about?*
Peter:	*No, I don't care what they are like, I just don't think they will be very nice to me.*

When his father asked him what worried him about the party, Peter's response was to give details of the situation that worried him, but what his dad really needed to know was what Peter thought was going to happen. He initially replied, 'I just don't want to go.' However, his dad then tentatively suggested possibilities to help Peter describe his fear. In Peter's case, his worry was different from what his dad had suggested but his dad making suggestions in a non-judgemental manner helped Peter to feel that his dad would understand when he found out what he was anxious about.

Making suggestions based on what you might get anxious about also shows children that it is not necessarily 'abnormal' to worry about a particular social situation. Other people are likely to worry about it too. Children often feel as if they are the only one who worries about a specific situation, but realizing that this is not true can make it much easier to talk about their worries.

But hang on, you may now be thinking, if I make suggestions to my child won't that just give them a whole load of new things to worry about? Our experience is that this does not happen. Children do not usually develop a new worry or fear just because someone has suggested it to them.

If your child finds it really hard to tell you what they are anxious about, which is common with shy and socially anxious children, it might be easier for them to write down their worries in a book for you to look at together or for you to read at a later date. Children often like keeping notes of their worries or anxieties and may spend hours decorating or making a special book to keep them in. Similarly, teenagers often keep personal diaries and so can sometimes see the benefit of keeping a record of anxious thoughts.

Sometimes children may report that they are not frightened of anything in particular, but that they are worried that they will get a frightened feeling. In this case, find out more about your child's thoughts about having this feeling. What if they do get that feeling? What would happen then? What is the worst that could happen? There are still likely to be frightening thoughts associated with the presence of this feeling, for example, I'll get a scared feeling and lose control and make a fool of myself, I will be sick and everyone will look at me and think I'm disgusting.

Checking that you've understood

If we already have an idea in our minds about what scares our child then it can be easy to draw quick conclusions about what they are telling us. To make sure you have absolutely grasped what is worrying your child you need to tell them what you understand from what they have told you, and give them the opportunity to correct you if you've got it wrong. Here is an example from Peter and his dad:

Dad: *Okay. I think I have a better idea what the problem is now but can I just check?*

Peter: *Okay.*

Dad: *The thing that makes you most nervous about going to Adam's party is that you think the other boys will say nasty things to you?*

Peter: Sort of.

Dad: Sounds like I haven't got it quite right.

Peter: I am more worried that they won't talk to me than that they will say nasty things.

Dad: Oh, I see. So the main thing is that if you go to the party, you won't have anyone to talk to.

Peter: Yes, I would have to sit on my own.

Dad: I see. That doesn't sound like much fun, I have to agree. So, you are worried that if you go to the party, no one will talk to you so you will end up sitting by yourself. Is that right?

Peter: Yes, that's right.

Dad: I see. I can understand why that might make you anxious.

A final point to make about Step 1 is that you will see, in the example given, that although Peter's dad is showing that he can understand why Peter is so worried, he does not ever say that it is right or wrong for Peter to be anxious. What he does say is that he can understand why Peter is anxious *given the frightening thoughts that he is having*. The implication here is that if Peter is going to be less anxious, something needs to be done about those thoughts.

Your child's thoughts

Have a go at completing the following figure for a social situation that your child finds anxiety-provoking. Your teenager may like to do this with you or may prefer to have a go on their own (see Appendix 6 for records for teenagers).

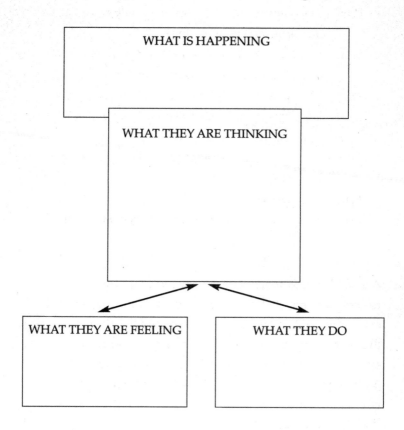

From this exercise we hope that the way your child behaves in certain social situations starts to make more sense. At times it may seem as if they are behaving irrationally, but when we take into account what they are thinking in that situation, their behavior is likely to make perfect sense.

Step 1

Key points

- Ask your child to express what is making them anxious during the social situation or as soon as possible afterwards.
- Make sure that the *way* you ask the question shows your interest and support.
- Keep an open mind about your child's thoughts. Don't assume you know what they are worried about.
- Keep questions 'open' too – use 'What' and 'Why'.
- If necessary make suggestions; what might worry you about this situation?
- When you think you have understood what your child is anxious about, check this out by repeating it back to them to make sure you have got it right.
- Help young children to express what they are anxious about, using dolls or stories.

10

Step 2: Is that a helpful thought?

Note: Read through all of Step 2 before trying to put any of the strategies into effect.

At this point, we hope that you now have a clear idea of what your child is thinking in the social situations that make them nervous. The next step is to set about helping your child to work out whether the thought is a helpful one, or whether there may be other ways of thinking about the situation that may be more useful to them in overcoming their shyness or social anxiety. This process is too complicated for young children and we will show you how to simplify it for this age group. In contrast, teenagers are often particularly good at challenging their anxious thoughts. In this section we will talk you through the basic steps. However, if you can be creative and find a way to make this apply to your child and their interests in particular, then they will relate to it and enjoy it more, both of which will increase your chances of success!

There are three steps for helping your child to evaluate their anxious thought. These are described in the box on the next page:

Steps for evaluating the thought

1 What is the evidence to support that thought?

Help your child to look for the evidence for the thought and work out whether this thought is (a) realistic or unrealistic, and (b) helpful or unhelpful.

Sample questions to ask

What makes you think that (the feared situation) will happen?

Has that ever happened to you before?

Have you ever seen that happen to someone else?

How likely is it that (the feared situation) will happen?

Tips to remember

Start with the thought that you think might be the easiest to change.

Work as a team: show your interest in what your child has to say.

If your child doesn't know what will happen encourage them to find out by setting up an experiment.

2 Considering alternative thoughts

Next you need to help your child to work out whether there are any other ways to think about this situation.

Sample questions to ask

Can you imagine that anything else could happen?

If (the feared situation) did happen, could there be any other reasons for it?

What would you think was happening if someone else was in the same boat?

What would (another child) think if they were in this situation?

Tips to remember

Give your child the chance to come up with helpful thoughts themselves.

If they need help, offer your child some suggestions to get the ball rolling.

Take all of your child's ideas seriously and praise their efforts.

3 Help your child to come to conclusions

So what does your child think now that they have considered different ways of thinking about this situation? Even if they still think something bad will happen, how likely do they think it will be? Your child may not draw the same conclusions that you might have, but this doesn't matter. The main thing is that your child has had practice at thinking about situations in other ways, besides the 'automatic' anxious way.

Tips to remember

It can be tempting to draw conclusions for your child, but try to hold back.

Thinking this through themselves will help your child to remember the conclusions and the procedure.

Thinking like a judge in court

The following stages can be likened to being in court. First, the alleged crime committed by the defendant (anxious thought) is outlined by the judge. Second, any evidence that supports the defendant's guilt is presented (evidence for the anxious thought), followed by any evidence against this theory (other ways of thinking about the situation). And lastly, the judge will decide if the defendant is guilty or not (is the anxious thought realistic or helpful?). These legal principles are often familiar to children, particularly teenagers, from television programs or films, so you may be able to take advantage of this to help to make the process appealing to your child. If not a courtroom drama, is there some other crime-fighting or problem-solving character who appeals to your child? If you are not sure, just ask your child who they would call in if they needed to solve a problem, or make tentative suggestions as Lauren's mum did in the example below. This is where your creativity comes in!

> Mum: Lauren, what's the matter?
> Lauren: Nothing. I just don't feel right. I really don't want
>   to go to school tomorrow.
> Mum: Well, you can't really miss school, can you? So,
>   we've got a problem that we need to sort out. Who
>   do you think could help us to solve a problem? It
>   could be anyone. It doesn't have to be a real person,
>   it could be a cartoon character or someone on TV or
>   in a book. Any ideas?

Step 2: Is that a helpful thought?

Lauren: What about Harry Potter? He always seems to sort things out.

Mum: That's a great idea. So let's imagine Harry Potter is here. I guess first he'll have to know what the problem is. So we'll have to tell him what it is about going to school tomorrow that bothers you. What shall we tell him?

Lauren: Ummmm…

Mum: Should we tell him that there is an important game of Quidditch tomorrow?

Lauren: Yes.

Mum: Is that what is worrying you about going tomorrow?

Lauren: No, I've got a maths test.

Mum: Okay, and what do you think will happen?

Lauren: I will make a mess of it.

Mum: I see. So we need Harry Potter to help us to work out if that really is going to happen. How could he do that?

Lauren: He could go into the future and look.

Mum: Maybe he could, or maybe he could look at the past? What has happened before when you had a maths test?

Lauren: I got lots of the answers wrong.

Mum: Okay. Has that happened every time you have had a maths test?

Lauren: No, only that one time. It was a really difficult test, the teacher said so.

Mum: And do you have really tricky tests a lot?

Lauren: *Not that often. Miss Blake said this one would be easier than the last one.*

Mum: *And do the other children get some answers wrong too?*

Lauren: *Yes, lots of them do. But a few really clever children don't.*

Mum: *Okay. We've told Harry Potter that you have a maths test tomorrow and that once, when you did a really tricky test, you got some answers wrong, but that most of the other children did too. Is that right?*

Lauren: *Yeah.*

Mum: *And if you do get an answer wrong, everyone will think you are stupid, or could something else happen? Harry needs to know if there are any other possibilities before he can decide what you should do. What would you think if one of your friends got an answer wrong?*

Lauren: *I'd think that the test was really hard, or maybe my friend was rushing a bit.*

Mum: *That's a good point. So what do you think Harry would say about going to school tomorrow when you've got a maths test?*

Lauren: *He might say that I will probably do okay, but even if I get some answers wrong, people won't think I am stupid as they probably got some wrong too.*

Asking questions, not giving answers

You will have noticed in the example above that Lauren's mum asked lots of questions to help Lauren work out other ways of thinking about the situation that she feared (see also Emily's example later in the section). This contrasts with the example below:

Dad: *Michael, what is it that worries you so much about going to Beavers?*

Michael: *I don't like it. The children might make fun of me.*

Dad: *Oh, come on, Michael. You'll be fine. Nothing happened to you at Beavers the first time you went; the children there were really nice.*

There are a number of reasons why asking your child questions to help them find a new way of thinking for themselves is likely to work out better than trying to talk your child out of their fear as Michael's dad does, although, of course, it is more time-consuming. The first is that if your child is able to think this through for themselves then they will be in a better position when something scary happens and you are not there. If they rely on you to reassure them, they are likely to panic when they need to act and think independently. Also, children remember what they have learned better if they were helped to work it out for themselves rather than simply being told. By having your help to think their anxieties through for themselves, this method of considering the evidence and alternative ways of thinking will become second nature to your child. Finally, as you can see from the example, asking children questions to help them think things through encourages them to get involved in fighting their own fears, and it puts them in a position of control (in contrast to feeling out of control which is common when people feel anxious). In contrast, just telling your child why they shouldn't think the way they do could encourage them to feel as if they are doing something wrong, are stupid and are being told off!

Practise first

It can be tricky to use questions in a gentle and interested way to help a child to think through their anxieties. We can easily be tempted to supply the answers or end up sounding judgemental about the answers they give us. For this reason before you have a go at this with your child find a willing volunteer to practise with, for example a partner, friend or relative. Ask them to imagine that they are your child and tell them which fear you would like them to pretend to have. Then work through the table 'Helping my child with "unhelpful thoughts"' at the end of this section with them. If you get stuck swap over and let your helper be you and you can be your child. See if this gives you pause for thought or any new ideas. Once you have had a practice, try this with your child. Don't worry if it doesn't go perfectly first time; it does no harm to show your child an example of practice making perfect! You can also practise these techniques with your teenager.

Test out the fears

Sometimes children may not really know what they fear will happen, they just don't like the idea of doing something, or they may simply have a bad feeling about it. They may not know whether the fear they hold is realistic or not, as they don't have any information to go on. At other times, your child may be able to think through their fear but end up feeling as if they shouldn't feel nervous, but still do. In all these situations help your child to put their fears to the test. Your child will no doubt be familiar with experiments from science classes at school. Your job now is to work with your child to design an experiment to find out if what they fear is true. For younger children, you may need to design these experiments for your child, while your teenager is likely to be good at coming up with their own experiments. Some examples are given below.

Experiments to test fears

1 **Francesca's mum will think I am stupid if I don't say anything when they come round**
Experiment: Do a survey and ask five people what they would think if someone came to play but didn't talk to their friend's mum.

2 **Everyone will make fun of me when I go to Beavers tonight**
Experiment: When you get home from Beavers, write down the name of everyone who didn't tease you.

3 If I don't do well in my maths test, I will get into big trouble

Experiment: Make one deliberate mistake on your maths test and record what happens.

4 If I ask a shop assistant to find something for me, they will think I am stupid

Experiment: Go to the shops with Mum/a friend and get her to ask the assistant for help. Record: (a) How stupid she looks; (b) What happens.

By setting up experiments and putting fears to the test your child's conclusions are more likely to really stick in their head. Using practical exercises like this will also help your child to *feel* differently, not just think differently.

A very important point to bear in mind is that if you set up an experiment with your child you *must* remember to ask them how it has gone and help them to work out what the results mean. Use the results to add information to the helpful thought record that you are working on with your child. Your child needs to feel that all their trouble was worth the effort and that it was a useful thing to do, especially if you ever want them to have a go at anything like that again!

Cutting out reassurance

Going through this process clearly takes more time than just saying, 'There's nothing to worry about,' 'You'll be fine,' or, even, 'Just get on with it.' Such responses may well be our instinctive reactions, but that approach seldom works. In fact, for shy and socially anxious children, reassurance can actually stop them being able to manage situations on their own. For example, a child who is always told, 'It's okay. Mummy's here,' can hardly be blamed for panicking when they run into problems when Mummy's not here! Reassurance is often a parent's natural reaction to their child's anxiety. But if your child is having problems with shyness or social anxiety, you must try to cut out the reassurance and instead use the questions to help your child to come up with helpful thoughts.

Actual and ongoing threat

A final, but important point to mention here is that as you become clearer on the details of what your child gets anxious about it may become apparent that there *is* an actual threat to your child. An example is a child who is scared to go to school because they are being bullied. For the child to feel differently about going to school, it is crucial that this problem is solved first of all. On discovering such a clear threat, it is vital that you take positive action to eliminate it. It makes no sense for a child to 'think positively' about bullying. However, even in a situation like this we would encourage you to involve the child in the problem-solving process, although the extent to which you can do this depends of course on the nature of the situation (Step 5 gives more information on involving your child in overcoming problems; Chapter 17, 'My child won't go to school', in Part Three talks specifically about bullying). If your child tends to think there is danger all around them and nothing can be done about it, when they do come across a real danger it is clearly important to show that in fact something can be done!

Simplifying the process for younger children

Younger children are likely to find the process of examining evidence and coming up with alternative ways of thinking far too complicated. What is essential for young children to learn, however, is that there can be different ways of thinking about the same situation. So the principle is the same as we have discussed above, although you will need to take a more active role to help your child to become aware of other ways of thinking.

More specifically, for younger children, you need to give your child suggestions of other ways to think about a frightening social situation, suggestions that will help your child to create a positive image of themselves coping with the situation. Using dolls, as we described in Step 1, bring in a new character and show how they would cope in the feared situation. Choose one of your child's favourite characters from television or books, and create a story in which this character overcomes the same fear (see 'Useful books and contacts' for a list of books for children about being shy or anxious). Importantly, this doesn't mean simply showing the character not feeling scared in the situation. Your child will relate to the story more if, just like your child, the character feels scared but doesn't let it stop them from having a good time. Use pictures and toys to illustrate this or build it into a bedtime story and this can then be used as a reminder when your child enters a similar situation. For example, 'Remember what Bob the Builder did?', 'Okay, Dora the Explorer, what are you going to do now?' Below is an example of a story that Rebecca's mum told her to show Rebecca that there were other ways of thinking about going to a party:

Mum:	*Dora the Explorer has been invited to Swiper's birthday party. There are going to be lots of other people there. How do you think she feels?*
Rebecca:	*Scared.*
Mum:	*Yes, that's right. Why do think she is scared?*
Rebecca:	*I am not sure.*
Mum:	*She feels a bit nervous as Dora won't know anyone except Swiper and she is worried that no one will play with her. But Dora didn't want to miss the party, so she decided to try to make herself feel a bit less nervous. Do you know what she did?*
Rebecca:	*No.*
Mum:	*Well, first she asked Swiper who was going to the party and guess what?*
Rebecca:	*I don't know.*
Mum:	*Well, Boots had been invited too so she knew two people who were going. So she felt less nervous.*
Rebecca:	*Yes.*
Mum:	*She also asked Boots if she could go with him. She asked him if she could call on him on the way so*

> *that they could walk to the party together and*
> *Boots agreed it was a good idea. Boots told Dora he*
> *was also a bit nervous and so he was pleased with*
> *her plan. Dora and Boots went together to the party*
> *and guess what? They had lots of fun. They met*
> *some of Swiper's friends who were really nice and*
> *Dora did have lots of children to play with and got*
> *a party bag to take home.*

With younger children you will also need to be more active in giving ideas of how to collect the evidence to examine anxious thoughts. Here's an example:

Rebecca:　*I don't like Amy (another girl at ballet class).*
Mum:　*Why don't you like her?*
Rebecca:　*She might be nasty to me.*
Mum:　*Has she been nasty to you before?*
Rebecca:　*I can't remember.*
Mum:　*Who could we ask to help us to find out? What*
　　　　about Mrs Grade, your ballet teacher?

Helping teenagers with anxious thinking

With teenagers, the process of asking questions, evaluating evidence and looking for alternatives can be really helpful. Here is a discussion between Emily and her mum:

Mum:	*What is it about PE that bothers you?*
Emily:	*Everyone will think I am really rubbish at it and will laugh at me.*
Mum:	*Let's try some of those questions in the book and see if they work!*
Emily:	*Okay. What makes me think it will happen? Well, that's obvious. I am awful at sports so they are bound to laugh.*
Mum:	*But has it happened before?*
Emily:	*Not to me, but to another girl.*
Mum:	*Does it happen a lot to this girl?*
Emily:	*No, only once, but it could happen again.*
Mum:	*What are the chances of that, do you think?*
Emily:	*Who knows!*
Mum:	*Let's try and work it out. How many PE lessons have you had with this girl?*
Emily:	*Loads, maybe 20.*
Mum:	*And how many times has she been laughed at?*
Emily:	*Once. Oh, I get it. So the chances of it happening again are only about 1 in 20, is that it?*
Mum:	*Yes, that was what I was thinking.*
Emily:	*But even with a small chance like that, it is not worth the risk.*

Mum:	Well, what would you think if someone laughed at your friend?
Emily:	I would think, 'Poor her', and I would try to comfort her.
Mum:	And so…
Emily:	My friends would do the same to me, I guess. They are good friends.
Mum:	So, is it so bad if someone laughs at you?
Emily:	It's not nice but maybe it is okay.

The written record

At the end of this step you will find a record form to note down how you get on with the tasks described, specifically:

a   What was happening that triggered your child's fear or worry,

b   How your child responded to your questions or experiments, and

c   The outcome – how your child thought, felt and behaved in the end.

Your teenager can keep these records for themselves (see Appendix 6 for records for teenagers). However, be sure to ask your teenager about them from time to time (although they may not want to show you them!) to show them that you are taking an interest and to motivate your child to continue with the records.

Step 2

Key points

- Show that you are interested in your child's point of view and take it seriously.
- Discover, with your child, what makes them have this thought.
- Help your child to consider other points of view.
- Help your child to conduct experiments to put their fear to the test.
- Hold back reassurance.
- Be creative and keep it fun where possible!
- For young children, suggest other ways of thinking and ways of testing out different ideas.

Helping my child with 'unhelpful thoughts'

What is happening?	What are they thinking?	Evidence and alternatives	What happened in the end?
	Why are you worried?	What makes you think that ___ will happen?	What did your child think?
	What do you think will happen?	Has that ever happened to you before?	What did your child do?
	What is this about (this situation) that is making you worried?	Have you ever seen that happen to someone else?	How did your child feel?
		How likely is it that ___ will happen?	

Step 2: Is that a helpful thought?

Can you imagine that anything else could happen?

If _____ did happen, could there be any other reasons for it?

What would you think was happening if someone else was in the same boat?

What would (another child) think if they were in this situation?

How could you test out this thought?

11

Step 3: Encouraging independence and having a go

Note: Read through all of Step 3 before trying to put any of the strategies into effect.

The first two steps have focused on anxious or unhelpful thoughts, in particular how thoughts can influence feelings and behavior. By now you will have discussed with your child what it is that worries them about specific social situations and you will have started to take some steps towards new ways of thinking about these situations. You may have found that your child has been able to think differently about their social fears and, as a result, they may have already begun to behave differently. For some children this can be the key step. For others, although they may be starting to think about the situation differently they still don't want to confront that situation. Maybe this isn't surprising if avoiding particular social situations is a habit they have had for a long time. In this step and the next we are going to talk about ways to encourage your child to have a go, rather than avoid social situations.

Encouraging having a go

As we have already said, if a person feels anxious they are more likely to try to avoid the source of their anxiety rather than confront it. In many ways this seems to be a sensible strategy. For example, if Lauren believes that by asking for help her classmates will think she is stupid or she will make a fool of herself, then it is not at all surprising that she won't ask. The difficulty is, however, that because Lauren never asks for help, she never finds out whether her belief is true or whether, in fact, her classmates won't even notice her asking. Reducing avoidance and learning to have a go is, therefore, crucial for overcoming shyness and social anxiety. Given your child's social fears, they are going to need some encouragement in order to have a go. The following strategies will help you to do this.

Attention and praise

Attention and praise are really powerful ways to influence children's behavior. Praise needs to be clear and specific so that your child understands exactly what it is that they have done that you are so pleased about. The following extracts from conversations between Lauren and her mum show examples of clear and specific praise.

General and vague
'Well done, Lauren.'
'Good girl.'
Clear and specific
'Lauren, you did really well today when you got ready for school so quickly and stayed calm despite the fact you

had a maths test today. I am really proud of you, you know.'

General and vague

'Mrs Jefferies said you were good in the play.'

Clear and specific

'Mrs Jefferies told me you were really calm before the play and despite being a bit nervous, you stood up and said all your lines. That is really great, you are getting so brave!'

Young children are especially sensitive to the messages they receive from their parents, so the principle of paying attention to desirable behavior is particularly important for them. Children learn that their actions have consequences at an early age; at less than two years old children recognize praise and will behave in a way that is likely to attract it. So we need to pay attention to children's positive, brave behavior when they are very young and respond to it with clear praise.

Distraction

If you praise brave behaviors, your child will learn that when they have a go and face their fears then good things happen. It is also important that they learn that when they are not able to face their fears *nothing bad happens*, but, at the same time, *nothing good happens*. When your child refuses to have a go or becomes anxious or distressed it would be wrong to ignore them completely, but what you can do is ignore the *fear* and ignore the *anxious behavior*. The simplest way to do this is to distract your child to help to take their mind off the fear, but without removing them from the situation (and encouraging avoidance). This is a particularly useful strategy for young children. So, for example, if your child becomes nervous as they approach the school playground change the conversation to point out something happening in the distance ('Wow, look at that cat'), talk about something good that will take place today, or what they would like to do after school. By using this strategy attention is not paid to your child's anxiety and they are helped to cope with their fear. The child also begins to discover that just because something seems scary at first it doesn't mean they can't deal with it, and they may even end up enjoying it! Here is an example of what Rebecca's mum did when Rebecca was anxious:

Mum:	*Rebecca, come and say hello to Sue.*
Rebecca:	*I don't want to (in a whisper).*
Mum:	*Why not?*
(silence)	
Mum:	*Sue and I are going to have a cup of tea and some of those nice cakes we made earlier. Do you want one?*
Rebecca:	*Yes please, in my bedroom (in a whisper).*
Mum:	*Do you want to help me decorate them?*
Rebecca:	*Yeah! (Rebecca comes downstairs quietly)*
Mum:	*Okay, what are you going to put on these cakes?*

	Smarties or hundreds and thousands? What do you think, Sue?
Sue:	Smarties. You are doing a good job there, Rebecca.
Rebecca:	Thanks.
Sue:	They're my favourite sweets, are they yours?
Rebecca:	Yes, I love chocolate (Rebecca and Sue chat for a minute or so).

(Sue leaves a bit later)

Mum:	Rebecca, I am really pleased with you. You talked to Sue so nicely, how brave is that? What about another cake as you have been so brave?
Rebecca:	Yes, please.

Being on the lookout for have-a-go behavior

Reducing the amount of attention you give to anxious behavior can be very hard as your child's upset or distress is likely to be your main focus. Michael's parents found it particularly hard to do this, as you can see from the example below.

You need to shift that balance and weigh attention more heavily on your child's attempts to face anxieties and, as we have already said, praise these at every opportunity. Although this all sounds simple enough, it can be quite difficult at times because it involves looking out for and noticing your child behaving in a way that might be taken for granted with another child. For example, we have heard about Michael's anxiety about going to Beavers. Every now and again Michael did manage to go to Beavers. As this was normal behavior for

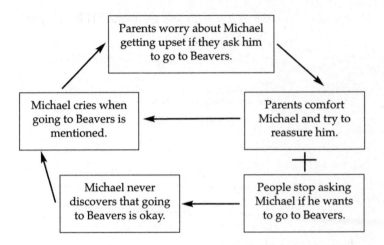

many children, his parents did not think to praise it. Once Michael's parents became more aware of this behavior, they had two other concerns about praising it. First, they worried that they might make Michael more aware that sometimes he was facing his fear, which might make it more of a big deal and make him more reluctant to do it. Second, Michael's brother was going to clubs regularly and he wasn't getting praise for doing so. Despite some reservations, Michael's parents praised Michael's efforts. They found that rather than Michael making a big deal out of going to Beavers, he really appreciated the praise and it seemed to boost his confidence. Michael's brother understood that Michael had difficulties going to Beavers so didn't feel he was being unfairly treated. In fact, he started to join in the praise himself. Michael's parents noticed that his brother was struggling with maths and started to give him lots of praise when he independently got started on his maths homework.

Rewards

In addition to praise when children achieve specific goals, giving rewards is an effective way of letting them know how much you appreciate what they have done and encouraging them to continue with that sort of behavior. Rewards don't need to be expensive; in fact they don't need to cost money at all. We are often struck by the rewards children suggest when asked to think of them. For example, Michael chose 'going to the park with Dad' and Lauren chose 'cooking with Mum' among their rewards.

Having a range of rewards to suit different achievements

You and your child will need to come up with a range of rewards to suit different goals. For example, if you were to give a huge reward for a small goal then what will you do when your child achieves a huge goal? On page 104 space is provided for you and your child to compile a list of rewards together. Only put down things to which you both agree. For instance, there is no point offering your child a trip to the cinema if they hate the cinema; equally there is no point setting up the trip of a lifetime as a reward if it is unlikely to happen!

Appropriate rewards

Try to think of rewards that you are able to give to your child immediately or very soon after they have made the achievement so that it is clear what has earned them the reward. For teenagers this is less important, as they are more able to wait for a reward. However, it is best not to wait too long in order to encourage them to tackle another problem. The rewards also need to be things that you will be happy *not* to give your child if the goal is not achieved. What would be the point of your child going to the trouble of overcoming their shyness or social anxiety if they could have got that reward anyway? An example of a reward that is not likely to work out is, 'If you can get to school on time every day this term we'll all go on a family holiday in the summer.' The first reason why not is that the promised reward is too distant in the future. It will mean they may have, for example, faced the fear for a whole week with nothing good happening as a result. Children are rarely able to see such a distant event as an incentive. Second, the holiday will probably need to be booked before the goal has been achieved and it will be very hard not to go should the goal not be met. This reward is also a very big deal! If your child had an even bigger goal to aim for in the future, how would you top that? Finally, the whole family's holiday resting on their performance puts a lot of pressure on the child and understandably siblings would be very annoyed if the family holiday was cancelled. The consequences of this are likely to be very negative for your child. Rewards, as we have discussed, act as a *bonus*.

Rewards for young children

Young children need instant rewards (e.g. stickers, sweets), something that you can give them the moment they achieve their goal. In general, children of three years and upwards will understand and respond to this type of reward. For slightly older children (four years or more), sticker or star charts can be used, where your child accumulates stickers or stars (which are themselves rewarding) for several days and then receives a small reward when they reach a particular target. The following are useful tips to remember when rewarding young children.

- Make sure your child understands what they will get as a reward if they have a go at a step on the plan ('If you manage to go to swimming club tonight, we can watch your favourite program when you get home').
- Be clear what they are getting the reward for ('Well done, because you managed to say hello to the lady at the check-out we'll go and make the cakes now').
- Reward your child every time they do each step, not just once.
- Give your child the reward immediately after they have completed the step (buy the reward beforehand so you have it ready to give your child, or make sure you have time set aside to do the rewarding activity with your child).
- Often with younger children, rewards that involve *doing* things with you are more effective than material rewards (i.e. making something rather than buying a toy).
- Give your child lots of praise as well for completing the step ('Well done for having your friend round, you were really brave and Daddy is very proud of you').

Rewarding teenagers

Although rewards may seem quite childish, they can also be a powerful way of motivating older children and teenagers. Their success depends on the choice of rewards. Of course, *you* must agree to the rewards before your teenager starts to face their fears so that they do not do so thinking they will gain something unrealistic, but it must be your teenager who makes the choice as only they know what will motivate them to face their anxieties. In contrast to younger children, doing things with you is often likely (but not always) to be less of a motivator, but coming up with ways in which you can facilitate activities that they can do with friends will provide good alternatives to material and financial rewards.

Praise and Rewards

Tips to Remember

- Make praise clear and specific;
- Include a range of rewards under each category;
- Rewards don't need to be expensive;
- Make sure both you and your child agree to the reward;
- Make sure you would be happy not to give the reward if the goal was not met;
- Try to have rewards that can be given immediately or soon after the goal has been met.

Rewards (things to do with my child):

_____

_____

_____

Other rewards (e.g. toy, money, football stickers):

_____

_____

_____

_____

Problems with giving rewards

Parents sometimes have concerns about giving rewards to their children. Some of the common concerns that parents raise are listed below, followed by our response to them.

Parents' concerns about rewards

1 I don't want to bribe my child to do what I want them to do

Sometimes parents feel as if they are manipulating their child by giving rewards and understandably feel this is wrong. We would agree that this is wrong if the child is being 'rewarded' for doing something that benefits the parent and not the child. Here, however, we are using rewards to help the child to do something specifically because it will benefit them in the future. As far as Lauren was concerned, asking the teacher for help could only have bad consequences (e.g. her peers would think she is stupid). Her mum, however, as an adult, was in a position to see that in the long term she would benefit academically from being able to ask for help when she was stuck. The reward her mum gave said, 'I know that was a really tough thing to do, so well done for doing it.' The promise of the reward really helped Lauren to face her fear as, in addition to the various negative consequences that she could imagine, there was now something clearly positive to be gained that would happen soon.

2 If I start rewarding this behavior I'll have to keep rewarding it forever

It is true that when you have identified a behavior as deserving a reward you do want to be on the lookout for it so that you can be consistent in rewarding it. As we have said above, however, rewards are used to help children to do something that would otherwise be difficult to face. Once that task becomes easy (or even boring) it no longer requires a reward, and it is time to shift the rewards to other goals (see Step 4 on taking a step-by-step approach). The end of a reward for a particular behavior can be framed as a positive thing, as Lauren's mum said to her: 'You're so good at asking for help in a small group now that I don't think we need a reward for that, do we? But remember, if you can ask a question to the learning support assistant in the big class, you will get a reward because it sounds like that is still quite hard for you.'

3 It is unfair on my other children who do this behavior without needing rewards

As we mentioned with regard to praise, children are able to understand that different children deserve rewards for different things as they each face separate challenges. One family we recently worked with had a great system in which the whole family earned rewards and whenever any one of them achieved their particular goal pebbles would be placed in a jar. When the jar was full the whole family would have a shared reward, such as a family outing!

4 Why should I reward 'normal' behavior?

Although the behavior you are hoping to see may be 'normal' for many children, for your child it is a struggle and they need help and encouragement. In fact the more 'normal' this behavior seems, the more upsetting it probably is for your child that they cannot do it as they may feel 'different' or 'freaky'. As well as motivating your child to have a go, the reward will boost their self-esteem by showing that you recognize their success.

Observing others' behaviors

As we discussed in Part One, an important way in which children learn to behave is by watching other people. Children can mimic how other people act so it is important to keep an eye on your own behavior and take every opportunity to show your child a good example of how to deal with your own anxiety or shyness. This does not mean covering it up. It means expressing your anxiety, acknowledging that it is possibly a 'fear' rather than an actual threat, considering alternative ways of thinking about it, and not letting the anxiety get in your way. This principle is particularly important for young children, who learn such a lot from observing those around them.

Observing others' feelings

Children also learn how to behave from how other people react to what *they* do in different situations. For example, Lauren's mum was very aware of her own anxiety about mixing with people she doesn't know very well. Although she was nervous about this, she didn't want to show it in front of Lauren as Lauren might learn from her that mixing with strangers was quite nerve-racking. However, Lauren was always looking for proof that mixing with others was scary (as we discussed in Chapter 5). So when Lauren's mum came to see Lauren's school play, she was worried that Lauren might get upset, and she knew that this would increase her own discomfort. And indeed Lauren did pick up on the changes in her mum's facial expression and thought that her mum's worried face was further evidence that mixing with the other parents was something to steer clear of.

At times, shy or socially anxious children can provoke deep worry or frustration in a parent. It is important to find ways to deal with these feelings so that they do not interfere with the work you are doing with your child. Additional principles 2, later in Part Two, focuses specifically on ways of managing your own anxiety to maximize the help you are giving your child.

Allowing independence

Your child needs to have the opportunity to develop independence, fight their own battles and make their own mistakes. Lots of parents, particularly those who have young children, talk about how hard it is to 'let go'. By this they mean letting their child become more independent, by going to nursery or school, leaving them with friends or relatives or encouraging them to do things by themselves. It can be particularly difficult if your child is very shy or socially anxious! Shy and socially anxious children often expect that they won't be able to cope in social situations and feel that they need to be protected by their parents. In turn, their parents protect them because they know how upsetting these situations might be. This means a vicious cycle develops, in which your child never learns that they can cope, nor how to cope.

Although the issue of letting go is probably more relevant to parents of young and, to some extent, primary school–aged children, as a parent of a teenage child you should also consider whether you are allowing your child enough independence, since it is at this age that they want more freedom. Are you giving your child an appropriate level of independence or not? It might be helpful to think about how much independence other young people of your child's age are given. However, don't feel pressurized to go beyond what you think is an acceptable level. Ultimately, as your child's parent, the decision is yours.

As parents of young and older children, you need to ask yourself whether you think you are putting in a lot of effort to try to protect your child or control the world around them. Could your child be learning from you that you regard the world as a dangerous place, and do you think that they can't manage on their own? If this is the case, you need to take a gradual, step-by-step approach to helping your child or teenager to confront their fears. This is the focus of the next step.

Have a go!

The table at the end of this step ('Responding to my child's shy or socially anxious behavior') is for you to record how you get on using the strategies we have discussed to encourage your child to face their social fears. As usual, we would encourage you to keep a record whether you feel it worked or not. This way, over time you will be able to see a pattern and will have a clearer idea which strategies work best with your child. On page 111 is an example of Lauren's mum's record. This shows how she responded to Lauren when Lauren had a headache before bed because she was worried about taking a test the next day. We would also encourage parents of teenage children to keep these records. You are likely to have less influence on your child than parents of younger children, but nevertheless it is important that you monitor how you respond to your teenager's shyness or social anxiety and try to do so in a helpful way.

Step 3

Key points

- Be on the lookout for your child having a go (and not avoiding their social fears).
- Praise and reward having a go.
- Set your child a good example of how you manage your own shyness or anxiety.
- Give your child clear messages that they can have a go and that they can cope!
- Use distraction with young children.

Step 3: Encouraging independence and having a go

Responding to my child's shy or socially anxious behavior: Lauren's example

Date	Behavior What did my child do?	Response What did I do?	Yes	No	Outcome What happened when I did this?
3 January 2007	Said she had a headache at bedtime and couldn't sleep.	Cut out reassurance.	YES		Lauren eventually got to sleep and went to school the next day without too much upset.
		Asked about anxious thoughts.	YES		
		Helped my child find alternative thoughts.	YES		
		Gave clear and specific praise.	YES		
		Offered a reward.			
		Showed how I managed my own fears about the situation.			
		Overcame my worries about my child in this situation.	YES		
		Stood back and allowed my child to have a go.			
		Cut out reassurance.			
		Asked about anxious thoughts.			
		Helped my child find alternative thoughts.			
		Gave clear and specific praise.			
		Offered a reward.			
		Showed how I managed my own fears about the situation.			
		Overcame my worries about my child in this situation.			
		Stood back and allowed my child to have a go.			

Responding to my child's shy or socially anxious behavior

Date	Behavior What did my child do?	Response What did I do?	Yes	No	Outcome What happened when I did this?
		Cut out reassurance.			
		Asked about anxious thoughts.			
		Helped my child find alternative thoughts.			
		Gave clear and specific praise.			
		Offered a reward.			
		Showed how I managed my own fears about the situation.			
		Overcame my worries about my child in this situation.			

Stood back and allowed my child to have a go.	
Cut out reassurance.	
Asked about anxious thoughts.	
Helped my child find alternative thoughts.	
Gave clear and specific praise.	
Offered a reward.	
Showed how I managed my own fears about the situation.	
Overcame my worries about my child in this situation.	
Stood back and allowed my child to have a go.	

For additional copies see Appendix 2

12

Step 4: A step-by-step approach to facing social fears

Note: Read through all of Step 4 before trying to put any of the strategies into effect.

Facing fears

One of the main ideas we have talked about so far is that to become less scared or worried about social situations we need to face our fears and find ways to cope with them. As we have already discussed, social fears won't go away unless we stand up to them. If we always avoid or run away from situations we are frightened of, we never find out whether they were really as bad as we thought or whether we could have coped with them. You will remember from the previous step that this is what happened to Lauren who never asked for help because she thought that if she did her classmates would think she was stupid.

By facing their social fears gradually, your child will find that they can tolerate more and more socially anxiety-provoking situations. This may be because your child, like Lauren, discovers that their fears are unfounded, or it may be that your child simply learns to put up with the feeling of fear without losing control or getting upset. As we mentioned earlier, in addition to seeing possible danger, your shy or socially anxious child may also feel that when confronted with danger they will not be able to cope. Facing fears can help your child to learn that they can, in fact, deal with these situations.

A step-by-step approach

To Lauren, the idea of asking the teacher for help was very scary. If we had just told her to get on and do this she probably wouldn't have followed our advice, and might have been left feeling quite hopeless about becoming less socially anxious. One way to make it easier to face fears is to do so step-by-step.

Making a plan

Drawing up a clear step-by-step plan with your child will help you both to focus on the goals you are aiming for. As a parent of a young child, you will need to devise the plan for your child, taking into account what you have learned about their social fears so far. For primary school-aged children, you can devise the plan together. Make it fun by being creative about how you present the plan and use characters and colours to decorate it, which will help your child to feel a part of the plan-making. Teenagers may well want to devise their own plan, and may wish to call it simply a ladder or hierarchy, but you should encourage them to share it with you so you can check with them that they have followed the guidelines outlined overleaf.

Create the structure for your plan first. For example, the plan could simply show a child moving up the steps of a ladder, or a rocket flying to the moon (stopping off at stars along the way), or a train going along a track (with the different steps marked at platforms on the way to the final destination), depending on your child's age and interests.

For teenagers, it could simply be a list of steps to be agreed on. There are five steps involved in making your step-by-step plan with your child as outlined in the box below.

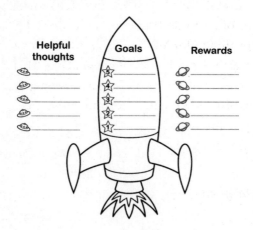

Example of an illustrated step-by-step plan.

Making a step-by-step plan

1 Identify your child's ultimate goal and ultimate reward.
2 List steps towards the ultimate goal.

3 Ask your child to rate the steps and put them in order from least to most scary.
4 Specify a reward to accompany each step.
5 Help your child to consider useful ways of thinking about the first step.

The ultimate goal

You and your child need to work out steps towards the ultimate goal. In order to do this, you first need to be clear about what you are aiming for. You will find it hard to work on your step-by-step plan if you have a vague goal like 'Be less worried in class', as how will you really know when your child has achieved this? To keep it clear and simple the goal needs to be something you (or somebody) can *see* your child do. Here are some examples of ultimate goals:

Ultimate goals

Rebecca: Go to a friend's house to play for half an hour while Mum goes off shopping.

Lauren: Ask the teacher for help in front of the whole class.

Michael: Go to Beavers once a week for a month.

Peter: Go to a party where there are some children I don't know and stay for at least an hour.

Emily: Eat my lunch in front of my friends at school every day for a week.

Manageable, realistic goals

As you can see, these goals all describe behaviors (rather than feelings). Try to think about it in this way; if your child was no longer anxious about this particular social situation, what would this mean they *could do*? Or, perhaps, it would be okay still to be a bit anxious, but what would they have to do to feel they have overcome the fear *enough*? For example, we could ask Lauren to go up to a complete stranger in the street and ask for directions but is that really necessary? Our guess is that not asking strangers for help is not causing Lauren a problem in her day-to-day life, whereas not asking her teacher for help is. We need to keep the goals manageable.

The goals also need to be achievable and realistic. If Michael could go to Beavers every day for a month, this would certainly be a test of whether he had overcome his fear, but Michael could never reach this goal as Beavers only takes place once a week! Similarly, if we asked Peter to go to a party where there were 100 people he didn't know very well, although this would be a great achievement, it seems scarcely necessary, as the chances of him ever having to attend such a big party where he knew no one are very slim. In summary, ultimate goals need to be clearly spelled-out behaviors that are achievable and realistic.

Two things that we have discussed in earlier chapters are going to be particularly important to help your child to have a go at each step. One is coming up with helpful thoughts about the step. The other is having the incentive of a reward. We will come back to helpful thoughts shortly.

Rewards

Alongside the ultimate goal, you and your child also need to decide on the ultimate reward! For Step 3, you and your child came up with a list of possible rewards. Now is the time to go back to that list and find a reward that fits such a big achievement as reaching the ultimate goal! Write this down on your step plan alongside the ultimate goal.

Ultimate Goals and Rewards

Rebecca

GOAL: Go to a friend's house to play for half an hour while Mum goes off shopping.

REWARD: Have a picnic tea in the garden with all my dolls.

Lauren

GOAL: Ask the teacher for help in front of the whole class.

REWARD: Decorate my bedroom.

Michael

GOAL: Go to Beavers once a week for a month.

REWARD: Day trip to a theme park.

Peter

GOAL: Go to a party where there are some children I don't know and stay for at least an hour.

REWARD: Trip to the cinema.

Emily

GOAL: Eat my lunch in front of my friends at school every day for a week.

REWARD: Buy a new pair of jeans.

Breaking it down into steps

Once you have your ultimate goal your task is to break it down into smaller, more manageable steps. We find it is useful not to have more than about ten steps so that your child is not overwhelmed and can see the end in sight. It can also be helpful to begin with a step that your child can already manage some of the time, so that the first step is fairly easy and makes an encouraging start to the plan. Here is an example of Lauren's step-by-step plan:

Lauren's step-by-step plan

STEP 1   Ask your friend for help after class
Helpful Thought: *I have done this before and it was okay. My friend didn't think I was stupid.*
Reward: *Praise from Mum.*

STEP 2   Ask your friend for help during the class
Helpful Thought:
Reward: *Buy an activity book.*

STEP 3   Ask the teacher for help after class when everyone has gone
Helpful Thought:

Reward: *Make some Christmas cards with Mum.*

STEP 4   Ask the teacher or learning support assistant (LSA) for help during small group work
Helpful Thought:
Reward: *Do cooking with Mum.*

STEP 5   Go up to the teacher during class and ask for help
Helpful Thought:
Reward: *Go on a shopping trip with Mum.*

STEP 6   Ask the LSA for help in class
Helpful Thought:
Reward: *Go to the cinema.*

ULTIMATE GOAL: Ask the teacher for help in front of the whole class
Helpful Thought:
Reward: *Decorate my bedroom.*

As we can see, Lauren's steps each build up towards the ultimate goal of asking for help in front of the whole class. The steps are ordered from the lowest to the most anxiety-provoking for the child. It's not always obvious which situations your child will find most frightening so it is important to ask your child what they think. In order to work out how to order the steps, ask your child to rate how scared they would be doing each step on a scale like the one on the next page.

0	1	2	3	4	5	6	7	8	9	10
Not at all			A little bit		Some		A lot		Very, very much	
☺										☹

Use the table below to think of steps with your child and ask them to rate how anxious they would be about performing each step.

How anxious does my child feel about doing each step?

Steps to include in my child's step-by-step plan	How anxious does my child feel in this situation?

Once your child has rated how anxious they would be when having a go at each step you can add them in order from the least to the most frightening to your step-by-step plan, or use the table on the next page. We find it is helpful to specify all the rewards for all the steps right from the start so that your child can clearly see what they are working towards and what they will gain along the way. However, be prepared to make changes if necessary. Your child may decide at a later date that something else would be more motivating, particularly if it takes some time to complete the steps.

Helpful thoughts

In Steps 1 and 2 you helped your child to come up with more positive, and less anxious, ways of thinking about their social fears. These strategies can be used now to identify what your child is worried will happen when they have a go at the next step, and to help them to work out if there are other (more helpful) ways of thinking about the step. There is no need to find helpful thoughts for all the steps at once, just focus on the step your child will be doing next as it is likely that your child will think quite differently about the ultimate goal once they have achieved some steps towards it. We have already seen, above, the helpful thoughts Lauren came up with for her first step. (*I have done this before and it was okay. My friend didn't think I was stupid.*) Once again, for young children, you will need to help your child to come up with more helpful thoughts for their step-by-step plan.

My child's step-by-step plan		
Goal	**Helpful Thought**	**Reward**
1 (EASIEST STEP)		
2		
3		
4		
5		
6		
7		
8		
9		
10 (ULTIMATE GOAL)		

For additional copies see Appendix 3

At the end of this step you will also be able to see the step-by-step plans of our other shy or socially anxious children, which will give you an idea of how a plan for a younger and older child might look.

Putting it into practice

So far this step has been about how to put together a step-by-step plan. It is now time for your child to take the plunge and try the first step in the plan. As we mentioned earlier it often works well to start with a step that you know your child can achieve, for example something that they have done once or twice before. Even though they have already done it, it is essential to give them a lot of praise so that they feel motivated to keep going with the step-by-step plan. Young children will need a lot of encouragement to complete each step while teenagers may want to carry out each step on the plan independently. However, it is still important to praise and reward your teenager for their efforts and to encourage them to move on to the next step.

Take your time

If the first step goes particularly well your child is likely to feel ready to rush on through the steps to their ultimate goal. We would encourage you, however, to slow down the pace a little. It is important that your child feels truly confident at each step before moving on to the next. Rushing ahead too quickly could lead to your child becoming very frightened by a step that they weren't ready for, losing confidence and wanting to give up the whole thing. Instead we like to see each step being *repeated* until your child feels confident enough to continue. Your child may still feel scared or frightened by the step, but this fear should no longer be overwhelming. It should instead feel manageable in order to continue with the step-by-step plan. Of course you may not be able to give the same reward repeatedly, but be sure to continue to praise the achievement and, perhaps, offer a smaller token reward to acknowledge it. However, as we outlined earlier in the tips for rewarding young children, they will need to be rewarded every time for their achievement and this reward needs to be instant.

Getting stuck into a step

Before your child attempts each new step go back to the principles you used in Step 2 about helping your child to change how they think and generate helpful thoughts. For example, Michael had successfully gone to Beavers to watch with his mum. He had his reward of playing a favourite game with his parents and was excited about having a go at the next step. However, when the time came, Michael still felt very scared. Opposite is the conversation that Michael and his mum had to enable him to come up with a thought that would help him to attempt the next step and then, because Michael was still daunted, they broke it down into smaller steps.

Step 4: A step-by-step approach to facing social fears

Mum: *Michael, how do you feel about this next step?*

Michael: *I don't want to do it.*

Mum: *What is worrying you about it? What do you think might happen?*

Michael: *I don't want to go to Beavers by myself. I won't know what to say.*

Mum: *What makes you think you won't know what to say?*

Michael: *I just won't!*

Mum: *Did you find it hard to know what to say when we went together?*

Michael: *No.*

Mum: *How did you know what to say?*

Michael: *I just did. But you were there and this time I will have to join in a lot of the stuff.*

Mum: *So you thought of something to say last time?*

Michael: *Yes. But I didn't have to join in so it was different I suppose.*

Mum: *Can you remember which of the children you talked to at Beavers when we went together?*

Michael: *Paul, Tom and Ben.*

Mum: *Okay, so if you go again, do you think you will be able to talk to them?*

Michael: *I guess I might but I am scared of having to join in too.*

Mum: *Okay. So it sounds like you think that you will probably be able to think of something to say to Tom, Paul or Ben because you did last time. Let's*

write down that thought as that sounds quite
helpful to remember. But I know you're still a bit
worried because you are going to join in some of the
things this time, although not the games. So how
about we make this a smaller step. Why don't you
go by yourself and we'll make sure that you don't
have to join in anything, or I come with you but
you join in everything except the games?

Michael: *Can I go by myself but not join in?*

Mum: *Good idea.*

Safety behaviors

Remember we talked earlier about safety behaviors, things that your child does to make themselves feel safe in social situations, and how they can prevent your child from confronting their anxiety completely, such as carrying a special toy, a bottle of water or wearing a hood to cover their face. Be on the lookout for safety behaviors that your child might adopt. Although, for example, having a bottle of water to sip might help your child to face a fear the first time, make sure that they do not become reliant on this prop. Next time make them repeat the same step without the water in return for an even greater reward.

When the step does not go well

If your child has a go at the step but it doesn't go as well as you'd both hoped it is still important to praise them for the attempt and trying to face their fear. It may just have been a bad day, in which case encourage your child not to give up but to try again as soon as they can, or perhaps some more planning is needed. For example, Lauren's step-by-step plan included Lauren asking her friend for help in the classroom. Lauren's mum wasn't sure whether Lauren would be allowed to do this so she needed to check it out with her teacher beforehand. Lauren's mum made an appointment to see the teacher to tell her about the plan that she and Lauren were following and also told her about the different methods that she had been using and, in particular, what she had found had helped Lauren the most (Chapter 20, 'Overcoming children's shyness and social anxiety: A brief guide for teachers', is designed to be copied and given to your child's teacher). Lauren's teacher was happy for Lauren to ask her friend for help and also promised that she would respond to Lauren in a positive way if she did ask for help (i.e. that she wouldn't say, 'Wait a minute') as she knew how hard it would be for Lauren to do so. Lauren's teacher also said that she would look out for any signs of progress that Lauren made and make an extra effort to praise Lauren for her efforts.

Michael's mum had to do the same at Beavers. She needed to check out that it was okay for her to attend with Michael, and that it was okay for Michael to attend without joining in. As well as teachers and club leaders, try to get on board anyone who may be able to help and encourage your child, for example family members and friends. The more praise and support your child receives the better they will feel about their achievements!

Rebecca's step-by-step plan

STEP 1   Have a friend round to play for an hour
Helpful Thought: *I have had friends round before and it has
            been okay.*
Reward: *Play a game with Mum afterwards.*

STEP 2   Have a friend and her mum round to my
            house for half an hour
Helpful Thought:
Reward: *Watch my favourite DVD.*

STEP 3   Have a friend and her mum round to my
            house for an hour
Helpful Thought:
Reward: *Do some painting with Mum.*

STEP 4   Pop into a friend's house with Mum and stay
            for ten minutes
Helpful Thought:
Reward: *Go to the cake shop on the way back and buy an
            iced bun.*

STEP 5   Go to a friend's house to play for ten minutes
            by myself while Mum sits in the car
Helpful Thought:
Reward: *Buy some of my favourite stickers on the way home.*

STEP 6   Go to a friend's house to play for half an hour
            while Mum sits in the car
Helpful Thought:
Reward: *Make some clothes for my dolls with Mum's help.*

ULTIMATE GOAL: Go to a friend's house to play for half an hour while Mum goes off shopping

Helpful Thought:

Reward: *Have a picnic tea in the garden with all my dolls.*

Michael's step-by-step plan

STEP 1   Talk to my friend Jack about what happens at Beavers and tell Mum and Dad about it

Helpful Thought: *It will be fine. We can play on my computer.*

Reward: *Praise from Mum and Dad.*

STEP 2   Go to the start of Beavers and enrol with Mr Baxter

Helpful Thought:

Reward: *Sweets after tea.*

STEP 3   Go to Beavers with Mum and just sit and watch

Helpful Thought:

Reward: *Play a favourite game with Mum and Dad when I get back.*

STEP 4   Go to Beavers and don't join in the games

Helpful Thought:

Reward: *Go to the park with Dad.*

STEP 5   Go to Beavers and stay for the whole time

Helpful Thought:

Reward: *Go swimming with Mum and Dad.*

ULTIMATE GOAL: Go to Beavers once a week for a
  month
Helpful Thought:
Reward: *Day trip to a theme park.*

Peter's step-by-step plan

STEP 1   Have a friend round for tea
Helpful Thought: *I have had friends round before and it has
                  been okay.*
Reward: *Watch football match on TV with Dad.*

STEP 2   Go to a friend's house for tea
Helpful Thought:
Reward: *Get favourite cake on the way home.*

STEP 3   Have several friends round for the afternoon
Helpful Thought:
Reward: *Choose a DVD to hire.*

STEP 4   Have several friends round and invite one
          child I don't know very well
Helpful Thought:
Reward: *Buy football magazine.*

STEP 5   Go out into town with two friends and one
          child I don't know very well
Helpful Thought:
Reward: *Go to cafe with Mum and Dad.*

STEP 6   Go to a friend's house with two other children I
              don't know very well and stay for the afternoon
Helpful Thought:
Reward: *Buy new football.*

STEP 7   Go to a friend's house for a sleepover with
              other children I don't know very well
Helpful Thought:
Reward: *Buy DVD of favourite film.*

ULTIMATE GOAL: Go to a party where there are some
                          children I don't know and stay for
                          at least an hour
Helpful Thought:
Reward: *Trip to the cinema.*

Emily's step-by-step plan

STEP 1   Go to a restaurant with Mum and Dad and sit
              in the corner
Helpful Thought: *I have done it before and it was okay; no
                          one will see me in the corner!*
Reward: *Watch favourite film on DVD.*

STEP 2   Go to a restaurant with Mum and Dad and sit
              in the middle
Helpful Thought:
Reward: *Go to the cinema with a friend.*

STEP 3   Invite my best friend to dinner
Helpful Thought:
Reward: *My best friend stays for a sleepover.*

STEP 4   Go to my friend's house and eat dinner with her parents

Helpful Thought:

Reward: *Go swimming with my friend the next day.*

STEP 5   Eat a burger in front of one of my best friends when we are in town

Helpful Thought:

Reward: *Get a new CD.*

STEP 6   Eat my lunch in front of my two best friends at school

Helpful Thought:

Reward: *Go to a concert with my friend.*

STEP 7   Eat my lunch in front of all of my friends at school

Helpful Thought:

Reward: *Get another CD!*

ULTIMATE GOAL: Eat my lunch in front of my friends at school every day for a week

Helpful Thought:

Reward: *Buy a new pair of jeans.*

Step 4

Key points

- Avoidance keeps social fears going.
- Help your child to face fears gradually.
- Draw up a step-by-step plan with your child or encourage your teenager to devise their own plan.
- Help your child to come up with helpful thoughts about the next step they face.
- Praise and reward your child's attempts at each step.
- If a step is too much too soon, break it down into smaller steps.
- Practise, practise, practise.
- Watch out for safety behaviors!

13

Step 5: Problem-solving

Note: Read through all of Step 5 before trying to put any of the strategies into effect.

Up to now, the emphasis has been on helping your child to think about social situations in a less anxious way and to have a go and face their social fears. Sometimes, however, your child may have good reason to see a particular social situation as frightening. For example, a child who is being bullied would understandably feel nervous about attending school. Although this is a genuinely difficult experience, you might be able to envisage this bullying happening to some children you know and who do not get quite so anxious as a result. What is likely to make a difference to a child's level of anxiety is their sense of how able they are to sort out the problem. As we have said in earlier chapters, children who are shy or socially anxious are more likely to think that they won't be able to cope with a situation and therefore to come up with solutions that allow them to escape the situation as quickly as possible (e.g. running away), rather than finding a solution that will stop this problem from happening again (e.g. sticking up for themselves). We want to help your child to be able to recognize when there is a problem and to feel confident about getting that problem solved.

The problem-solving strategies we will discuss are particularly useful for teenagers. Adolescence is a time when your child should be becoming more independent and one part of this process is for them to be able to start dealing with tricky situations by themselves. The problem-solving steps we describe below are a good way of starting to do just this. These strategies can also be used with young children. However, as with the previous steps, they will need much more guidance than other children. At the end of this step, we have outlined ways of adapting this technique to make it more effective for each of these age groups.

When problem-solving is needed

Sometimes problems may emerge while you are investigating anxious thoughts with your child. For example, if your child feared being bullied you would probably ask, 'Has anything like that happened to you before?' If you then discovered that it had, and was even still happening, then this would clearly require positive action. By using problem-solving you can work with your child to decide on the best course of action (for more information on dealing with bullying, see Chapter 17, 'My child won't go to school', in Part Three).

Problem-solving may also be useful if your child reaches a step on their plan that requires some organizing in advance. For example, one of Michael's steps was to go to Beavers but not to join in the games. However, Beavers was cancelled that week as the club leader was ill, so Michael and his parents used problem-solving to work out what Michael could do instead.

Another situation in which problem-solving can be useful is when you and your child have gone through the methods described in Step 2, to consider how your child is thinking about a feared social situation, and your child has concluded that the feared situation is not very likely, but it *is* still a possibility. You will remember from Step 2 that as well as interpreting situations as threatening, shy or socially anxious children also tend to see themselves as being unable to deal with any threat that they might come across. Problem-solving can be useful to help your child work out either how to deal with a problem that does arise (as above) or to take control and prevent a problem arising.

As a parent of a shy or socially anxious child, you have probably noticed that your child sometimes comes home from school upset about something. On further discussion, it becomes clear that a problem has arisen at school and your child is not sure how to deal with it. It might be a problem with friends, or with schoolwork or with a teacher. Whatever the problem, this is another opportunity for your child to use the problem-solving strategies that we talk about below.

Becoming an independent problem-solver

When a child is shy or socially anxious, it can be very tempting to try to solve their problems for them. A good example would be going into school to sort out a problem that has upset your child, as we mentioned above. As parents, we want to do all we can to stop our children from becoming upset. But if your child is going to feel confident that problems can be solved, whether you are there or not, then they need to learn how to solve problems for themselves. This doesn't mean that your child can't ask others for help. Asking for help can be a good strategy for solving many problems (and is often essential, for example in a bullying situation), but it is your child's responsibility to consider this solution among other possibilities and come to a decision about the best way forward.

Step-by-step problem-solving

Once again there is a series of steps involved in becoming an independent and effective problem-solver. The steps we describe may seem familiar to you, as many adults will use these steps automatically when they are faced with a problem. The steps are: (1) being clear about what the problem is, (2) thinking of as many solutions as possible, (3) weighing up the pros and cons of each solution to decide which will be the best. Following these steps will help your child to be clear about what they need to do to develop this new skill. Eventually the steps will become second nature to you and your child and it may not be necessary to sit and work through them all one by one, but to get to this stage we would encourage you to stick with the steps until solving problems in this way becomes a habit.

Keeping records

At the end of this step you will find a 'Problem-solving' table to fill in which will guide you and your child through the steps. There is also an example of a table that Lauren's mum completed. We would urge you to use the table and keep a written record of your child's attempts at problem-solving as (a) having it written in front of you keeps it simple as there is less to remember, (b) it makes the process that you are working through really clear to your child, and (c) should the same problem happen again in the future then your child can look back at the table to see what can be done. Once again, your teenager may prefer to fill in the charts for themselves (see Appendix 6 for records for teenagers).

What is the problem?

It seems obvious, but the first step is to find out what the problem is. The only way to be completely clear about this is for your child to describe the problem to you. You cannot assume that you know what it is. When your child has told you then use your own words to check with them that you have understood. Whether you think this is a genuine cause for concern or not, it is clearly worrying your child so it deserves your understanding, but let's keep it quite matter-of-fact. We want to get across to your child, that, yes, you can see that they are worried and that there is a problem to be solved. So how is it going to be solved?

Opposite is an example of a conversation that Lauren and her mother had before a new LSA started in Lauren's class.

Step 5: Problem-solving

Mum: Lauren, why don't you want to go to bed? You have been much better at it lately. Is something wrong?

Lauren: I have got a headache.

Mum: Why is that, do you think?

Lauren: I'm worried about tomorrow. Do you remember I told you that Miss Smith, our LSA, has left. Well, the new one starts tomorrow, Mrs Cox. She is from another class and they say she is horrid.

Mum: What do you think is going to happen?

Lauren: That she will ignore me if I ask for help or say that I have to ask the teacher.

Mum: What would you do then?

Lauren: Go bright red. All the children will laugh at me.

Mum: It sounds a bit like the worries you had before about asking for help. You have got much better though, haven't you? How have you dealt with these worries before?

Lauren: I know. I know she probably won't ignore me or get cross with me for asking but I can't be sure as I don't know her and everyone says she is horrid.

Mum: I see your point. So you think that if you ask for help, the new LSA will ignore you and all the children will laugh. Let's see if we can think of some ideas to sort this out.

Weird and wonderful solutions

Your child may find it difficult to come up with solutions to problems; after all, maybe until now they have avoided dealing with problems; or maybe problems have all been sorted out for them. Whatever the reason, this step is all about helping your child to get into the habit of finding solutions. At this point we don't care what the solutions are, or even if they would work, we just want solutions and lots of them! Coming up with a solution, any solution, deserves praise and every idea should be taken seriously. The fact that your child is having a go at thinking of ways to overcome problems is a positive and important step!

If your child really struggles to come up with any solutions, as young children are likely to do, then you may need to give gentle prompts (or in the case of young children, suggest possible solutions yourself). For slightly older children, try to ask questions rather than offering solutions. For example, 'What would someone else do in this situation?', 'When this happened before, can you remember what you did then?' Or if more is needed, 'I know someone who had this problem and they did … Do you think you could do anything like that?' Opposite is the conversation that Lauren and her mother had to try to come up with as many solutions as they could to solve the problem of Lauren having a new LSA in the class-room who wasn't aware of Lauren's difficulties and whom Lauren thought might ignore her or get cross when she asked for help.

Lauren:	*Can't I just stay at home tomorrow?*
Mum:	*Okay. That is one idea. What other ideas can we come up with?*
Lauren:	*Get rid of Mrs Cox.*
Mum:	*It's an idea, I suppose! Any more?*
Lauren:	*No.*
Mum:	*You have had supply teachers in the past. What have you done when you've had one of them?*
Lauren:	*You've written them a note about my problems.*
Mum:	*Good, that's another idea. Can you think of any more? After all, you are very brave these days, so what could you do?*
Lauren:	*What do you mean, like talk to Mrs Cox myself?*
Mum:	*Another excellent idea.*

Which is the best solution?

Your child needs to learn how to choose which is going to be the best solution to try. In order to do that they need to consider:

1   What would happen (in the long and short term) and

2   How practical (or do-able) the solution is.

As you are taking all the solutions your child has come up with seriously, go through all the ideas one by one (even the seemingly silly ones) to find out what would happen and whether that solution would be doable. Some sample questions are listed below to get your child thinking about the consequences of each solution.

Sample questions

- What would happen if you did …?
- What would happen in the end?
- Would it make any difference to what would happen in the future or if this problem came up again?
- How would that change how you would feel if this problem came up again?

Your child may not be used to thinking in this way, in which case you may need to prompt them again gently. As before, try to stick to asking questions rather than giving answers to help your child to think about this for themselves. You will see an example of this in the conversation between Lauren and her mum below.

Mum:	*We've got lots of different ideas here, well done! So let's think about what would happen if you did each of these things. Your first idea was to stay at home. So what would happen if you stayed at home?*
Lauren:	*I wouldn't see Mrs Cox so it would be fine.*
Mum:	*That's true. What else would happen? What would Miss Smith say?*

Lauren:	*Nothing, you could say I was ill.*
Mum:	*But Mrs Cox will be there every day. Can you miss school every day?*
Lauren:	*I guess not.*
Mum:	*And what do you think would happen if you did?*
Lauren:	*I'd get into trouble.*
Mum:	*Yes, and how would you feel about Mrs Cox?*
Lauren:	*Pleased not to see her but I guess I would still be scared of her.*
Mum:	*Yes, I agree. Let's write all this down so we don't forget. Now let's look at the next one, 'Get rid of Mrs Cox.' What would happen if you chose that one?*
Lauren:	*I don't think I could get rid of Mrs Cox, it's not my job! Shame, though!*
Mum:	*Let's just say you did. What would happen if you got another LSA?*
Lauren:	*They might be scary too!*
Mum:	*Good point. What about your next idea?*

Lauren's responses to her mother's questions about the other solutions are all shown in the sample table at the end of this step.

Once your child has considered the possible outcomes they need to think about whether it is actually going to be possible to carry out this solution. Some sample questions are given in the box below:

Sample questions

- Is this solution possible?
- So would you be able to try this solution?
- Is there anything that would make this solution difficult to carry out?

With all this information, your child can then decide how good each solution is. By giving a number to each solution it is then easy to compare them and choose the best ones. Your child should by now be accustomed to using a rating scale. Use the one below to rate how good each solution is:

0	1	2	3	4	5	6	7	8	9	10
Not very good					OK					Brilliant
☹										☺

As in all the exercises, try to hold back your judgement and allow your child to decide how good each solution is for themselves. After all, if you decide that it is great, but your child has reservations then they are not going to be very motivated to give this solution a try.

Make a decision and have a go!

Once the possible solutions have been rated, taking into account the consequences and the practicalities, it will be easy to see which will be the best one to try. Before they get started, check with your child that they have everything they need to put the plan into action. Have a practice run or do a role-play first. Does your child need to get anyone else to help?

How did it go?

After your child has had a go you need to check how they got on. If the plan of action did not work out as well as your child had hoped, help them to think about whether there is anything they could do differently next time. Or is it worth trying another one of the solutions that they came up with? But do remember, no matter how it went your child deserves praise for having a go at overcoming a problem.

Adapting the problem-solving process for teenagers

Initially, you will also need to go through these steps with your teenager, in order to teach them how to problem-solve. However, once they have got the hang of these, they can do it more independently. Your child should be able to come up with a list of possible solutions and be able to rate them in terms of how good they are and how doable they are. They may want to check with you whether their preferred solution is a good one and it is important that you remember to ask them how they got on with putting their solution into action so that you can praise their efforts.

Using problem-solving with younger children

For your young child, you will need to help them to come up with different solutions as they may find it hard to generate more than one or two ideas. You can get your child to rate the solutions for how doable they are, but use a very simple rating scale, rather than the one shown above, as children under 7 years old can find this type of scale difficult to understand. You could, for example, simply ask your child whether each idea is a 'good', 'medium' or 'not a very good' idea. You will also need to help your child to think about the possible consequences of each solution by asking them specific questions about each one (e.g. what would happen if you...?). You may also need to help your child to carry out the chosen solution and then you can talk together about how well it worked. For example, Rebecca came home from ballet class one day very upset. She said she couldn't do a particular ballet step and so didn't want to go back again. Opposite is a conversation between Rebecca and her parents.

Rebecca: I am not going again. It is too hard. I can't do it.

Mum: It would be a shame never to do ballet again as you are really good at it. Let's try to think of an idea to help us in this tricky situation. What could you do?

Rebecca: I don't know.

Mum: Could you talk to Mrs Faulkner?

Rebecca: I don't want to.

Mum: Could you do it with our help?

Rebecca: I think so.

Mum: What about doing extra practice?

Rebecca: Maybe.

Mum: Have you got any ideas?

Rebecca: I don't want to go again.

Mum: That's an idea too so we have got three ideas. Let's see how good they are. So is not going to ballet again a good, medium or bad idea?

Rebecca: Good.

Mum: Are you sure? You wouldn't see your friend Chloe again.

Rebecca: Medium.

Mum: What about extra practice? Good, medium or bad?

Rebecca: Bad, really bad.

Mum: Okay, one left, talking to Mrs Faulkner with Mum and Dad's help?

Rebecca: Good.

Mum: So which is the best idea, which one is good?

Rebecca: Talking to Mrs Faulkner, but only if you help me.

Step 5

Key points

- Help your child to define the problem clearly.
- Encourage your child to come up with as many solutions as possible or, for younger children, offer suggestions.
- Ask your child questions to get them to think about the consequences of each solution and how practical it is.
- Ask your child to rate each solution and choose which is the best.
- Recognize the step your child has made to become an independent problem-solver.

Step 5: Problem-solving

Problem-solving: Lauren's example

What is the problem?	List all the possible solutions	What would happen if I chose this solution?	Is this plan doable? Yes/No	How good is this plan? Rate 0–10	What happened?
I am scared that the new LSA will ignore me if I ask for help, or get cross with me and tell me to ask the teacher.	1 Stay at home.	1 I would have to miss school every day to avoid Mrs Cox and I would get into trouble for this. I would still be scared of Mrs Cox.	Yes	2	I told Miss Smith I wanted to tell the new LSA about my plan and she was really pleased. She asked Mrs Cox to come and talk to me, which she did. She was very nice and helped me in the lesson.
	2 Get rid of Mrs Cox (LSA).	2 Not really possible. I'd still be worried about the next new LSA.	No	1	
	3 Mum to write a note to the LSA.	3 I would go to school. The LSA might be nice to me. If I had any problems with future teachers, I would need Mum to sort it out. Mum can't always help.	Yes	7	
	4 Lauren to talk to the LSA about her step-by-step plans.	4 I would go to school. The LSA might be nice to me. I would be very nervous about talking to the LSA. The LSA would be pleased that I spoke to her and would think I was brave to be doing a step-by-step plan. Mum might give me reward for being brave.	Yes	8	

Problem-solving

What is the problem?	List all the possible solutions No matter how weird or wonderful	What would happen if I chose this solution? In the short term? In the long term? To my anxiety in the future?	Is this plan doable? Yes/No	How good is this plan? Rate 0–10	What happened?

153

14

Additional principles 1: Helping your child to be socially skilled

Note: Read through the whole of this section before starting to put the strategies into effect. This section also requires you to have read the preceding sections of Part Two.

Why are social skills important?

Does your child know how to behave in social situations? Do they know how to talk to other children and adults? Do they know what to do if someone asks them to do something they don't want to do? Do they lack confidence in their ability to get on with other people? Some shy or socially anxious children do not know how to do these things; they have not learned the skills needed to interact with others in a comfortable and confident way. For example, Peter finds mixing with other children and adults hard. Although he plays with his cousin, he usually does what his cousin says as he is unsure what to say or do. When his mum's friends come round, he does not know what to say to them, so he stays quiet. At school, he tries not to talk to the teachers as he does not know what to say or how to ask for help. Other children are able to interact with other people perfectly well but these children think that they are really bad at it.

It is important that your child has both the confidence and the skills to deal with the social situations that, hopefully, you are now encouraging them to confront, having read the guide. If your child does not have some or all of these skills, or lacks confidence in using them, this chapter will assist you to help them to develop them.

It is possible to help your child become more socially skilled and socially confident at any age. Young children are still in the process of developing their social skills so this is the perfect time to help them to learn about interacting with others by using the strategies below. As with previous strategies, your young child will require considerable guidance and we will tell you how to simplify these techniques accordingly. Helping your teenager to improve their social skills or social confidence is also important. If they enter into adulthood with poor social skills or lacking in confidence socially, they are likely to find lots of situations difficult to deal with. Many jobs, for example, require good social skills. The strategies discussed below are all appropriate for use with teenagers. However, once again, you will need to allow your teenager to take the lead and we will guide you in adapting the way you work with them. In particular, you can increase your teenager's social confidence by noticing and praising them when they interact well with others.

How can I tell if my child is socially skilled?

On the following page is a list of questions that will help you to decide if your child needs assistance with their social skills.

You may want to go through these questions together with your child, although try to do so in a sensitive way as they may feel criticized if you highlight lots of skills they are not very good at. It may simply be a boost in confidence in using social skills that your child needs. Your teenage child may wish to answer these questions by themselves (see Appendix 6 for a self-report version of this questionnaire). However, you should encourage them to share their conclusions with you so that you can help them to use the strategies below. Discussing the answers with your teenager will also be a good opportunity to give them positive feedback about the skills that you think they are quite good at.

Non-verbal skills

1 Eye contact
   Does your child look people in the eye (without staring) when they are interacting, rather than looking down or away?

2 Posture
   Does your child stand or walk in a confident way, for example standing upright and walking with their head up and shoulders back?

3 Voice
   Does your child talk at the right volume and at the right speed? Do they talk clearly, rather than mumble?

Verbal skills

4 Greeting people
Does your child say hello and goodbye to people, or do they just look down or ignore them?

5 Talking to people
Does your child ask questions or say something to the other person, to start or keep a conversation going? Do they answer other people's questions and listen to what they have to say?

Friendships

6 Taking the initiative
Does your child invite other children to play or to come round for tea? Do they ask to join in other children's games or activities?

7 Feelings
Does your child offer to help other children if they are in trouble or need assistance? Is your child kind to others who are feeling sad or upset?
Does your child compliment their friends or family or praise them?

Assertiveness

8 Asking for help
   Does your child ask for help from adults or other children if
   they need it?

9 Sticking up for yourself and others
   Does your child say 'no' if they don't want to do something
   that another child asks them to do?
   Does your child stick up for other children if they need help?

10 Saying what you think
   Does your child say what they think, even if others might
   not like it, but in a way that does not upset others?

You will probably find that your child has some of these skills but not all of them, in which case, read on. You can help your child to develop specific social skills that they are lacking by following the strategies on the next page. Some children with shyness or social anxiety will have very few of these skills and will need a lot of help to learn how to interact better with other people. These strategies are designed to assist you to help your child to develop a whole range of social skills. It may take some time but if you and your child persist, you are likely to be successful. However you may decide, having answered the questions above, that your child does, in fact, have good social skills. In this case, there may be no need to implement the strategies outlined (although you should read the final section on creating social opportunities for your child). Instead, concentrate on tackling other social situations that your child currently finds hard, with the confidence that your child does have the skills to deal with these situations appropriately. Nonetheless, before you do so, remember that many shy and socially anxious children have the necessary skills to interact with others but are not confident in their own ability to socialize. These children think they are bad at interacting with others, whereas, in fact, they have good social skills. Talk to your child about how they rate their social skills. If they are not confident about their ability to interact with others, despite having good social skills, it is important that you work through the strategies outlined in 'How do I help my child to become more socially confident?' later in this section.

How do I help my child to become more socially skilled?

Using the questions above, identify which specific skills you think that your child is currently lacking and choose one that you and your child would like to work on first. As before, your teenage child is likely to want to make this decision for themselves, but may want your guidance. Follow the four steps on the following pages until you feel that your child has really started to develop the new skill that you both identified. As always, try to make it as fun as possible!

1 Gather information

Your child needs to learn exactly how to execute a particular skill. For example, if you and your child have decided that they need help with improving their eye contact when they are talking to other people, your child needs to know where they should look when someone is talking to them. They need to know that they must look at the other person when they are talking, but should glance away every now and then so that it doesn't seem as if they are staring. They should not look down or away while the person is talking. Show your child what to do by example and encourage your child to watch your use of eye contact, either at home or when you are out. You can also point out other people doing it. For example, get your child to watch their favourite TV characters or soap opera and look at how they use eye contact when they are talking. People-watching is a particularly appropriate strategy for teenagers who may not wish to take your advice about how to interact with their friends! However, you can still point out good examples to them. For young children, you need to teach them a very simple skill, such as saying hello or answering when someone asks them a question, rather than something more complex such as being assertive.

2 Get your child to practise their new skills

Once your child has a clear idea of what they should do in a particular situation, you can encourage them to practise what they have learned so that you can check if they have understood. The easiest way to do this is to perform a role-play together. You can be the teacher whom your child needs to talk to and they can be themselves! Remind them what you said about eye contact and watch how they get on. Don't interrupt during the role-play; wait until the end. Teenagers may feel uncomfortable engaging in a role-play with you. If so, see if you can find someone else with whom they might be more willing to do this exercise, perhaps a friend or a sibling. Once again, for a young child, keep your role-play simple and repeat it as many times as you can to ensure that your child has understood what they need to do so that they remember it for real-life situations.

3 Praise your child for their efforts

Praise your child for their attempts even if you think they made a real mess of it! Make sure you spot the things they did well and give them lots of praise for this, for example, 'You definitely looked me in the eye a few times, well done!' Try to keep focused on what they did well, so as not to knock their confidence by pointing out all the bad bits. If you think they didn't get the hang of it, gently tell them why and suggest how they can do it even better next time; for example, 'You tried really hard, and looked at me a few times. Great! But I did notice you kept looking down. Can you try again and keep looking at me this time?' Keep practising until they are confident that they have got it right. Try to make it as fun as possible, perhaps by pretending to be other family members, friends or TV/film characters. You also may need to reward your child for their efforts in order to keep them motivated and interested. You can see the benefit of your child learning social skills but they may not be able to! Remember too that rewards for young children need to be as instant as possible.

4 Encourage your child to practise the skills elsewhere

Once you feel that your child has got the hang of the new skill, using role-play, get them to practise in real-life situations. So, for example, they could practise their eye contact when they have to talk to the teacher or even just chatting to friends. You can use a step plan, as we talked about in Step 4, to come up with a list of situations in which your child could practise their new skill. With young children, you may want to be present when your child practises their new skill, such as saying hello. You can then gently remind your child what to do if they forget and can give them immediate praise for their efforts.

Peter and his mum agreed that he could do with some help with using eye contact, talking to people, taking the initiative and being assertive. They decided to work on talking to people first. Below is an example of how Peter's mum helped him to decide what he needed to do when he spoke to people.

Mum:	*Okay, so talking to people is hard.*
Peter:	*Yes, when they say something to me, I don't know what to say back.*
Mum:	*Right, when does this usually happen?*
Peter:	*At school. One of the boys might come up to me and say, 'You all right, mate.' I don't know what to say so I stay quiet.*
Mum:	*I guess you could say, 'I'm very well, how are you?'*
Peter:	*No, that sounds daft.*

Mum:	*Fair enough. I guess it would be good to answer the question though and then ask him a question.*
Peter:	*Yes, I could. What could I say though?*
Mum:	*How about… 'I'm all right, mate, how about you?'*
Peter:	*Yeah, that would be okay. What next?*
Mum:	*If he says okay, you could ask him what lessons he has had.*
Peter:	*That's boring.*
Mum:	*What would someone else ask in this situation do you think?*
Peter:	*I don't know.*
Mum:	*What about, what is he doing at lunchtime or did he see the Arsenal/Spurs match last night?*
Peter:	*That's a better idea. What if there was no match?*
Mum:	*You could ask him which team he supports.*
Peter:	*Yeah, I could.*

As you can see from their conversation, Peter and his mum worked out exactly what Peter could say when someone talked to him. And Peter watched his mum when they were out and saw what she said to other people she met. He also asked his cousin for ideas. Once they had done this, Peter and his mum practised together. His mum pretended to be a boy at school and Peter was himself. In the role-play, Peter asked the boy lots of good questions and his mum praised him for doing such a good job. Peter went to school the next day and practised his new skill when a boy came up to him. He managed to ask him a few questions and the boy asked a few back. Peter was really pleased with how it went and came home and told his mum, who gave him lots of praise. They then thought of some other situations in which Peter could practise talking to other people and they made a step plan so they had a clear course of action.

Rebecca and her mum also identified some skills that Rebecca needed to work on. One of them was what to say when Rebecca met someone. Below is a conversation between Rebecca and her mum. You will notice that Rebecca's mum gives Rebecca a lot of guidance on what to say when she meets other children and adults, although she does try to get Rebecca to notice what others do in this situation too.

Mum:	*So, the first thing we need to do is decide what you should do when you first meet someone, maybe a friend or an adult.*
Rebecca:	*Okay.*
Mum:	*Any ideas?*
Rebecca:	*No.*
Mum:	*What do I do when I see Mrs Faulkner at ballet?*
Rebecca:	*Say hello.*
Mum:	*Excellent, so you could say hello too.*
Rebecca:	*I guess.*
Mum:	*What do the other children at ballet say to each other?*
Rebecca:	*Not sure, maybe, 'Hello, I like your new ballet shoes.'*

Mum: *Good one.*

Rebecca: *Or, 'Can I stand next to you today?'*

Mum: *Another good one. Okay, so when you see Mrs Faulkner at ballet you need to say, 'Hello,' and when you see the other children you can say, 'Hello,' and you can also say, 'Can I stand next to you today?' or, 'I like your ballet shoes.' Let's have a practice.*

Tips for teaching your child good social skills

- Choose one skill at a time to work on (e.g. eye contact).
- Make sure you explain to your child exactly what they need to do.
- Give your child lots of opportunities to see you or other people doing it first.
- Give your child lots of time to practise with you to build up their confidence.
- Get your child to practise in real-life situations and report back to you as soon as possible so that they can remember how it went.
- Give your child lots of praise for their efforts.

How do I help my child to become more socially confident?

If your child has good social skills but believes that they are bad at mixing with others, you need to help them to become more socially confident. Below are some strategies that you can use with your child to do just that.

Giving attention to good social interaction

Try to be on the lookout for times when your child interacts well with others, for example instances when they look someone in the eye when they are talking to them, say hello to someone, or listen to what someone else is saying. Also include interacting with you or other members of the family. Your child will probably not be aware that they interacted in a positive way so it is important that you point this out to them. As we talked about in Step 3, it is helpful to give your child specific praise so that they know what they did that was good. The more often you are able to point out to your child good examples of their social skills, the more they will begin to believe that they can, in fact, interact well with others.

Challenging thoughts

If your child is socially unconfident, they are likely to have anxious thoughts about their behavior in social situations. For example, Lauren was due to go to a holiday club where she didn't know any children. She had lots of anxious thoughts, including, 'I won't know what to say to the other children, I won't know how to ask how to join in with their games,' and 'If they are nasty to me, I won't know what to say.' However, Lauren's mum had answered the questions earlier in this section about her daughter's social skills, and had found that Lauren did, in fact, have good social skills. Lauren's thoughts were, therefore, unrealistic and Lauren and her mum set about trying to challenge them. Use Steps 1 and 2 to help your child to identify any anxious thoughts they have about their ability to interact with others and to help them to challenge these.

Testing out the fears

You can also help your child to challenge their anxious thoughts about their social skills by encouraging them to put these to the test by carrying out experiments. Using experiments can be a really helpful process. For example, Lauren and her mum decided to test out Lauren's fears about not knowing what to say to the other children at the holiday club and not knowing how to join in. Lauren's mum asked the organizers if she could attend the first session of the holiday club so that she could observe Lauren's behavior. Beforehand, Lauren and her mum agreed that Lauren's mum would rate how good Lauren was at talking to other children and how good she was at joining in (on a scale of 1 to 5). Lauren also rated how good she thought she would be and Lauren's mum asked the club leader to do the same thing. Afterwards, Lauren and her mum compared the ratings and Lauren found that both her mum and the club leader rated her as good at talking to the other children and good at joining in. This gave Lauren some clear evidence against her anxious thoughts that she would not know how to talk to the other children or how to join in.

Another way of helping your child to collect evidence about their social skills is to videotape them interacting socially, and for you both, and other people if possible, to rate your child's social skills. Your child is likely to find that other people's ratings are higher than their own. It is, of course, not always possible for you or other people to observe or record your child interacting with others. Instead, you can help your child to begin to evaluate their own performance by getting them to describe to you what they did, rather than how they felt. Your child is likely to have felt very nervous but this does not mean that they did not interact well with the other person(s). Ask them what they said and what they did. Get your child to tell you how the other person responded; for example did they nod, stare, look interested, smile? Help your child to evaluate the evidence they present to you in order to decide if their anxious thoughts are realistic or not. Once again, do praise your child for any examples they give you that indicate that they interacted well with the other person(s).

Being assertive

One of the most important social skills children need to learn is to be assertive. Assertiveness is about being able to stick up for yourself in difficult situations without being aggressive. One situation that many children find hard to deal with, particularly those who are shy or socially anxious, is being picked on or bullied by another child. In this type of situation, children tend to respond in one of three ways, as shown below.

Being passive, assertive or aggressive

A boy is being called names by a child at school. What does he do?

Passive

He looks down and tries not to get upset. When challenged, he quietly says, 'I don't care anyway, say what you think.' He doesn't say anything else and when the child pushes him, he runs off.

Assertive

He looks the boy straight in the eye and says, 'Don't say that, it is not very nice.' He tells him he doesn't like it and that he will go and get some help if the bully doesn't stop. The child says it again and he responds, 'You've made me cross, you are not being fair. I am going to get someone to sort this out.' He walks off calmly to talk to the teacher.

Aggressive

He gets really cross and says, 'I hate you, shut up.' He calls the child some names back and when the child pushes him, he hits him several times. He says, 'You're stupid and I am going to get you.' He hits him again and throws some stones at him.

How do you think your child would behave if they were teased? Children who are shy or socially anxious are most likely to respond in a passive way, although a small number of children might act aggressively. Being assertive is a really useful skill for shy or socially anxious children to help them in a variety of difficult social encounters. You can help your child to work on being assertive by using the four steps outlined earlier in the chapter. When Peter was more confident about talking to people, he and his mum decided he needed to work on being more assertive. Peter and his mum first discussed what Peter should do and say when someone called him a name. He also watched his mum and dad in situations when they had to be assertive, for example taking something back to a shop. You can see below how Peter and his mum practised this new skill using role-play. His mum played the boy at school who was calling him names. After a few practices, Peter really got the hang of it. All he had to do now was to try out his new skills at school.

Mum:	*Who do you think you are, weirdo?*
Peter:	*I am not weird. So please stop calling me that (Peter looks the boy in the eye when he is talking).*
Mum:	*Oh yeah, you reckon. Don't argue with me otherwise I will belt you.*
Peter:	*Oh yeah. I've not done anything to you and it will get you into trouble (Peter tries hard to keep looking at the boy and to stand upright).*

Mum:	*So you're going tell on me, are you? God, you're sad.*
Peter:	*If you call me that name again, I will go and tell someone and you will get in big trouble, be warned.*
Mum:	*Oh yeah. Think you're big, do you?*
Peter:	*I'm bigger than you. You only do this 'cos you're not very confident. Why don't you try and be nice to people for a change? You might make more friends that way.*
Mum:	*Forget it (boy walks off).*

Providing your child with social opportunities

In order for your child to practise and improve their social skills, they need to engage in a variety of social activities. Certainly, children get lots of opportunities to mix with others at school and this is one of the most important reasons for going to school. However, at school, shy or socially anxious children commonly mix with the same friend or friends every day so their social opportunities are restricted. Your child will benefit from mixing with a whole range of children and adults, some of whom they might know better than others. They will learn social skills from watching and interacting with others and engaging in these activities will also increase their confidence about being in social situations. On the next page is a list of child-friendly social activities. Have a look and see how many your child currently does.

Social activities for children

Clubs run at school in lunchtime and after school (e.g. music, karate).

Sports clubs.

Beavers, Brownies, Guides, Scouts, etc.

Swimming lessons.

Dance classes.

Music lesson/choir.

Having a friend to tea.

Going to friends for tea.

Having a sleepover.

Having a party.

Mixing with parents' friends and their children.

Playing outside with other children.

Doing a school play.

Holiday clubs or schemes.

Spending time with relatives and cousins.

Calling for a friend on the way to school.

If your child engages in none or only a few of these activities, it would be worth discussing with them what else they could do. They might feel nervous about doing more of these activities, in which case you might need to develop a step plan to help them to overcome their anxiety about them.

Giving younger child lots of social opportunities

It is important that you encourage your young child to engage in a variety of social activities so that they can develop good, confident social skills as they are growing up. You can give your child the best chance of doing so if you make sure that they have contact with other adults and children and engage in both formal social activities (such as clubs or playschool) and informal ones (such as having a friend round for tea, paying for something in a shop or talking to your next-door neighbour).

Social activities for teenagers

As with younger children, your teenager also needs lots of social opportunities. As you are well aware, you may not, of course, be able to dictate what they do! However, you can make suggestions or offer to help, for example, by giving a lift somewhere. You may find you become a glorified taxi service but this also has the benefit of providing a chance for you and your teenager to have a one-to-one chat in the car so that you can make sure they know how well you think they are doing. Below is a list of the types of social activities that your teenager might be interested in.

Social activities for teenagers

Having a friend round for the evening.
Going to a youth club.
Going to a sports club or drama club.
Going into town with friends.
Dance lesson.

Having a sleepover or go to a sleepover.

Having a party or go to a party.

Getting a part-time job (that involves mixing with other people).

Going to a concert with friends.

Helping your child to be socially skilled

Key points

- Identify with your child what social skills they need to work on.
- Talk to your child about how to perform a particular skill.
- Get them to practise the skill with you and then in real-life situations.
- Teach your child to become more assertive.
- Make sure your child is engaged in several social activities out of school.

15

Additional principles 2: Managing your own anxiety

Note: Read through the whole of this section before starting to put the strategies into effect. This chapter also requires you to have read the preceding parts of Part Two.

As we discussed in Chapter 4, there are likely to be several factors that have led to your child becoming shy or socially anxious. It doesn't really matter what originally *caused* your child to be anxious or shy. What does matter, however, are any factors that may be keeping the shyness or social anxiety going, or getting in the way of you and your child overcoming their shyness or social anxiety.

Often parents of children who are socially anxious or shy are themselves socially anxious or shy, like their child, while others might experience different types of anxiety. These can include generalized anxiety (excessive worry), specific phobias (fear of a specific object or situation, e.g. spiders) or panic attacks. When anxious children with anxious parents receive treatment for their anxiety, they often do much better if the parent's anxiety is treated first. There are two likely reasons for this. First, if you are less anxious your child will start to learn other ways of thinking and behaving from you. Second, if you are less anxious you are likely to find it easier to follow this program.

If you are an anxious person yourself, a concerted effort to overcome this will not only help yourself but also your shy or socially anxious child. In this section we will first talk about methods of tackling your own anxiety. These strategies can be used for all types of anxiety not just social anxiety. For more extensive advice on overcoming your own anxiety problems or shyness you may find it useful to read other titles in this series (see 'Useful books and contacts'). We will then discuss specific ways in which your own anxiety may impact upon your attempts to help your child and how to overcome these.

Being aware of your own shyness or anxiety

As we discussed earlier, experiencing anxiety is normal, and happens to everyone. The point at which it becomes a problem, however, is when it starts to get in the way of your life: your work, your friendships, your family and your parenting. If you recognize that anxiety is stopping you from doing things you would like to do then it is important to address it. Similarly, many adults are shy and, as we have already discussed, shyness can be a positive trait. However, when shyness stops you from engaging to the full in activities or experiences, it is time to do something about it.

Use the space provided opposite to write a list of anxieties or shy behaviors that you feel interfere with your life.

My own anxieties

1 _____

_____

2 _____

_____

3 _____

_____

4 _____

_____

5 _____

_____

6 _____

_____

The strategies that have been discussed in this book are not used exclusively with children or young people, but are very similar to ones that adults can use. While we do recommend a number of books aimed at adults to help them to overcome their shyness and social anxiety, other types of anxiety or difficulties with mood or feelings (see 'Useful books and contacts'), there is no reason why you cannot use the strategies and skills that you have learned in this book. To recap, the following box summarizes the main strategies we have focused on.

Overcoming your own shyness or anxiety

1 Overcoming your anxious thoughts

How are you thinking about situations and people that you come across? Are you expecting the worst? Seeing danger all around you? Would other people think about these situations differently? What is the evidence to support how you are thinking? Is there any evidence to suggest you could think differently? How can you test out whether your thoughts are realistic? On page 180 you will find a similar table to the one you used with your child in Step 2. This time try out the chart to consider one of your own worries or anxieties. First, of course, you need to get a clear idea of what your anxious thought is. Then you can consider the evidence for or against your thought. On the basis of this do there seem to be other ways of thinking about this situation?

2 Overcoming avoidant behavior

Are you keeping away from the things that scare or worry you? How can you come to face the fear gradually? Make your own step-by-step plan. Reward yourself for your progress and encourage others to reward you too!

3 Overcoming problems

Do you feel paralysed when confronted with a problem? Instead try to focus on solutions. What are all the possible things you could do (no matter how silly)? What would happen if you did these things? What will be the best solution? Give it a try and see how it goes.

By overcoming your own anxiety or shyness, you will make it much easier for both yourself and your child when it comes to helping them to overcome their shyness or social anxiety. We will now turn to some of the specific ways in which you being less anxious or shy will encourage your child's progress.

Encouraging helpful thinking

In Step 2, you helped your child to discover new, helpful, ways of thinking about social situations that they feared. As we discussed in that section, anxious children and anxious adults both tend to think about things in a similar way: seeing situations as threatening, feeling unable to cope with that threat, and anticipating that they will become really distressed. In Chapter 4, we talked about how children learn from watching others. Seeing a parent think about the world in this negative way may encourage a child to do the same.

On the other hand, if a parent can set an example to their child of thinking about things in a helpful way, this will show the child a new way of seeing the world that they can learn from. This is quite different from a parent trying to cover up their anxieties. Children often say that they feel as if they are the only one who feels the way they do, and they feel like a freak for being scared all the time. Often they are not aware that *everyone* has anxieties and that *everyone* feels scared sometimes. Rather than hiding all your anxieties from your child it is important to show that having anxiety is normal and that there are ways of dealing with it so that it doesn't take over your life.

Helping myself with 'unhelpful thoughts'

What is happening?	What am I thinking?	Evidence and alternatives	What happened in the end?
	Why am I worried?	What makes me think that _____ will happen?	What did I think?
	What do I think will happen?	Has that ever happened to me before?	What did I do?
	What is it about (this situation) that is making me worried?	Have I ever seen that happen to someone else?	How did I feel?
		How likely is it that _____ will happen?	

Can I imagine that anything else could happen?

If ___ did happen, could there be any other reasons for it?

What would I think was happening if someone else was in the same boat?

What would someone else think if they were in this situation?

How could I test this out?

For additional copies see Appendix 5

The way that anxiety is talked about and responded to makes a big difference to whether children adopt the anxiety for themselves. For example, Michael knew that his mum had a fear of spiders. Michael's mum explained to him: 'It's just me being silly; spiders are harmless and most people don't mind them at all.' Because Michael had never been told to keep away from spiders and had, in fact, been encouraged to pick them up, he knew that they were not harmful and so, despite his mum's fear, Michael did not share her anxiety about spiders. Michael's mum talked to him in a sensible way about her fear, which also helped. How you discuss your anxieties with your child is important. In particular, they need to be talked about as 'just' anxieties or worries rather than as facts. To help you to think about your anxieties and whether they are 'just' fears as opposed to facts, try out the strategies we discussed in Steps 1 and 2 yourself.

Of the anxieties that you are challenging, you may want to select one that is appropriate to share with your child (e.g. a fear of cats or a fear of doing a presentation at work in front of the whole office; not something of an adult nature, such as money or relationships worries). Your child may be able to help you to go through the chart, asking you the questions, which will make your child feel more and more of an expert when it comes to helpful thinking!

Worries about your child

Having a child is worrying! Having a shy or socially anxious child is more worrying! Having a shy or socially anxious child when you are already an anxious person yourself is clearly not going to be easy. It is normal to worry about your child, but, as with all worries, if they are getting in the way of parenting your child in the way that you would like to then they need to be tackled. If your child is aware of the extent to which you worry about them, they will not want to be open with you about their own worries for fear of upsetting you further. You need to be able to show your child that you can deal with worry and anxiety.

What do you expect of your child?

As we have said, shy or socially anxious children do present a worry to their parents, but if a parent already tends to be very anxious this is likely to be amplified. We have found that parents who think in an anxious way usually expect their child to see the world in a similar way. How a parent thinks about their child will, of course, influence how they behave with their child.

If you think your child is going to get very upset, you are naturally going to want to do what you can to prevent this. You may want to remove them from the situation and reassure them that they will be all right. On the other hand, you may expect that they are going to make a big fuss and you feel annoyed or irritated and become snappy or cross with them. Although both of these reactions are completely understand-able given how you are expecting your child to react, they are both likely to get in the way of the work you are doing to help your child to overcome their shyness or social anxiety.

Lauren's mum, like her daughter, found social situations hard and worried about what other people thought of her. She found dropping Lauren off at school quite nerve-racking as it involved standing with the other mums. She often felt she did not know what to say. It was worse on the days when Lauren had tests, as she would sometimes cry when her mum dropped her off. Lauren's mum found this really embarrassing and thought that the other mums would think that she was a bad parent. She got so anxious she sometimes forgot how to help Lauren keep calm about the test. Instead, she found herself getting cross with Lauren and this just made things worse.

Anxious signals: giving negative information

Both your own worries and your worries about your child can sometimes 'leak out', and be visible to others. You need to be on the lookout for subtle expressions of anxiety when you are with your child. Ask a friend, partner or relative to watch you when you encounter a stressful situation with your child. Can they help to you spot whether your anxious feelings are apparent and getting in the way of you helping your child? For example, despite maintaining a calm manner, do you cross the road whenever a dog approaches? Or, despite being hospitable to your new neighbours, do you still express relief when they have gone home? These are examples of ways in which we unwittingly display signs of our own anxiety.

We talked earlier, in relation to Step 3, about Michael's parents who were really worried that Michael might become upset and not be able to cope if he went to Beavers. Michael picked up on the changes in his parents' expressions when they mentioned going to Beavers and interpreted these as more evidence that going to Beavers was, indeed, something to be feared. What we expect our children to fear and how we expect them to cope with threat is influenced by how we, ourselves, think about threat. Furthermore, our expectations of our children are likely to influence how we behave around them (particularly at times of fear or stress) and this may influence how our children actually cope. This creates another vicious cycle:

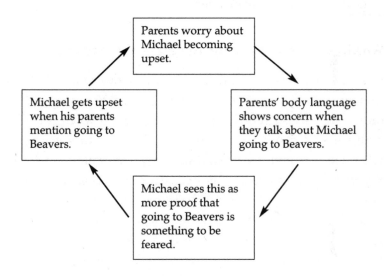

Parents worry about Michael becoming upset.

Parents' body language shows concern when they talk about Michael going to Beavers.

Michael sees this as more proof that going to Beavers is something to be feared.

Michael gets upset when his parents mention going to Beavers.

Both Lauren's mum and Michael's mum and dad sat down and completed tables to see if they could find another way to think about their children and their fears. What they came up with is shown on pp. 186–8.

Helping myself with 'unhelpful thoughts': Lauren's mum's example

What is happening?	What am I thinking?	Evidence and alternatives	What happened in the end?
I am waiting outside school with Lauren before class starts.	**Why am I worried?** Lauren is going to make a fuss when it is time to go in as she has got a test today.	**Has that ever happened to me before?** Yes. When she has a test she gets upset. I don't know what the other mums are thinking. **Can I imagine that anything else could happen?** Some test days Lauren doesn't cry, she just looks really sad and is grumpy. I could praise her for going in nicely or buy her something after school to show I am pleased and that might make a difference.	**What did I think?** Other mums are probably sympathetic, thinking, 'Poor woman, she has a tough job'. I thought, I can try a new strategy, I can really praise Lauren if she goes in without crying when she has a test and I can buy her a magazine or something small when she comes out.

What is it about this situation that is making me worried?

She'll get upset and cry.
Everyone will look at me and think I'm a bad parent.

Have I ever seen my fear happen to someone else?

When Lauren was younger, quite a few of the children got upset at the beginning of school.

What would I think was happening if someone else was in the same boat?

I would think they had a tough job.

Can you imagine that anything else could happen?

Well, I suppose other parents might think I had a tough job, which I do!

What did I do?

We decided to do a step plan for going to school and used the rewards as it says. Lauren tried really hard and has definitely got a bit better.

How did I feel?

I felt much better. Having something to work on really helped. I knew what the plan was and I reminded myself that other parents probably weren't thinking bad things about me.

Helping myself with 'unhelpful thoughts': Michael's mum's example

What is happening?	What am I thinking?	Evidence and alternatives	What happened in the end?
We have just had a call from one of Michael's friend's mums asking if Michael will go to Beavers with her son.	**Why are we worried?** Michael will get upset and refuse to go. **What do we think will happen?** We will keep asking him but he won't go. It will put us all in a bad mood. We'll also worry about what we says to his friend's mum.	**What makes us think that this will happen?** Michael hates going to Beavers and hasn't been for ages. **Can we imagine that anything else could happen?** Michael has been to Beavers in the past. We are working on his plan but we haven't got to this stage yet. **If it did happen, could there be any other reasons for it?** He may get upset because he has fallen out with a child at Beavers recently. He is also a bit poorly. **What would we think was happening if someone else was in the same boat?** We would support them so the child did go to Beavers even if only for a bit.	**What did we think?** It doesn't matter if Michael gets upset. We can continue to use our step plan to tackle his anxiety. **What did we do?** We told Michael we were confident he could go to Beavers when he had done the easier steps and reminded him of his reward. **How did we feel?** Nervous but Michael was okay. So we hope he will go to Beavers by himself soon!

Anxious signals: giving positive information

Being positive about your child's attempts at facing their shyness or social anxiety can be more difficult for a parent who themselves feels anxious or shy. For example, mothers who feel anxious in social situations tend to look concerned when their child interacts with a stranger. Children pick this up and become more worried themselves by the presence of a stranger. Feeling anxious when your child is in a situation that would scare you may relate to what you are expecting to happen to your child or how you are expecting them to feel, as we discussed above. It is important to recognize these thoughts and expectations so that they don't get in the way of your being able to support your child in facing their fears in a fun and relaxed way. Use a thought record to challenge thoughts that are making it hard to feel truly positive about your child facing their fears.

Do as I do

Your child won't just pick up how you react when *they* face their shyness or social anxiety. They will also pick up how *you* react to the social situation yourself. If a child sees their parent dealing with anxieties by trying to avoid them then it is likely that the child will learn to do the same. On the other hand, if a parent can show their child that they are able to face anxiety and overcome it then this will serve as encouragement to the child. If you see your child's shyness or social anxiety as a problem, but do not perceive your own as an issue, you are inadvertently giving your child a mixed message. The message your child gets is: you need to deal with your shyness and social anxiety, but I don't need to tackle mine. Tackling your own shyness or anxiety may not be easy but it is fine for your child to see that you too are experiencing difficulty, as they will also undoubtedly struggle at times to overcome their shyness or social anxiety. The same tips that we provided in Step 4 may be useful for you in overcoming your shyness or anxiety, in particular taking a gradual, step-by-step approach.

Getting your child involved

Again, your child may be able to help you to draw up your own step-by-step plan and may even be able to reward you for your achievements. Getting your child involved in this way can be good for a number of reasons: (1) it shows your child the strategies you are using to overcome your anxiety, (2) it puts your child in a position of control and being the 'expert', (3) having someone to push you along will help your motivation, and (4) it will make it all more fun! Remember to refer back to the first four steps in this section for tips on generating helpful thoughts, rewards and step-by-step plans.

Opposite is an example of the step-by-step plan that Lauren and her mum came up with to overcome Lauren's mum's anxiety about going to yoga class.

Lauren's mum's step-by-step plan

STEP 1   Practise yoga video at home
Helpful Thought: *This will be really good for me and if I practise I will be okay before I even go to the class.*
Reward: *Praise from Lauren.*

STEP 2   Practise yoga video with a friend at home
Helpful Thought:
Reward: *Praise from Lauren.*

STEP 3   Take a friend to yoga class and pick her up, chat to others at the end
Helpful Thought:
Reward: *Cup of tea made by Lauren.*

STEP 4   Go to yoga class and just sit and watch
Helpful Thought:
Reward: *Lauren will help with housework.*

STEP 5   Go to yoga class with a friend, sit and watch, and chat to others after class
Helpful Thought:
Reward: *Peaceful bubble bath with no interruptions.*

STEP 6   Go to yoga class once with a friend
Helpful Thought:
Reward: *Make cake with Lauren.*

STEP 7   Go to yoga class once by myself
Helpful Thought:
Reward: *Breakfast in bed made by Lauren.*

STEP 8   Go to yoga class with a friend every week for
          a month
Helpful Thought:
Reward: *Trip to cinema with Lauren.*

ULTIMATE GOAL: Go to yoga class by myself every
                    week for a month
Helpful Thought:
Reward: *Night out with friends (Lauren with babysitter).*

Creating the right opportunities

From the examples in the step-by-step plans in this book, it is
clear that we can't always just wait for the right situation to
arise for a child to be able to overcome their shyness or social
anxiety. If we want them to face the problem, and in a gradual
manner, we need to create the opportunities to enable them to
do so. This may mean liaising with a teacher (as we saw in
Lauren's plan, Step 5) or other people who may be able to help
(such as friends, as Lauren's mum did in order to overcome her
anxiety about yoga class).

As we know, Lauren's mother also felt anxious in social situations, in particular those where she felt others were judging
her. Approaching Lauren's teacher was, therefore, quite a difficult thing for her to do, as was asking a friend to help her with
her anxiety about yoga class. Here is another area, then, where
it is important to be aware of whether your own anxiety or
shyness could get in the way of your efforts to help your child

to move forward. If it is, then maybe the task you need to undertake to help your child could form the ultimate goal for your own step-by-step plan?

Encouraging problem-solving

If your child sees you spending a lot of time getting anxious or worrying about certain social situations, then they are not seeing you solve problems in constructive ways. You need to use problem-solving for your own anxieties in order to encourage your child to do the same. By doing this you will be helping yourself, and also showing your child a constructive way to deal with problems.

If this isn't enough

Reading through this section, you may have recognized your own thoughts and behaviors and you may now have tried out the strategies discussed for yourself. You may feel, however, that the anxieties that you experience, social or otherwise, are too great to tackle on your own. In this case you may find it helpful to seek professional support in overcoming these diffi-culties. Your general practitioner can advise you on how to obtain this sort of support locally. At the end of this book you will find 'Useful books and contacts' which includes reading materials in this series as well as information on organizations aimed at adults suffering from emotional difficulties. In our experience, where parents are able to overcome their own anxieties this helps them enormously to assist their child to overcome their own.

Managing your own anxiety or shyness

Key points

- If a parent is shy or anxious, this can make it more difficult for them to help their child to overcome shyness or social anxiety.
- Let your child know that everyone experiences some anxiety sometimes.
- Demonstrate to your child how you deal positively with anxiety or shyness using helpful thinking, step-by-step plans and problem-solving.
- If anxiety about a situation is stopping you creating opportunities for your child to face fears, then set overcoming this anxiety as your own ultimate goal.
- If further help is needed do not be afraid to ask for it. It could benefit both you and your child.

16

Some final words on the guide: Keeping it going

We hope that you are now feeling more and more confident about applying the strategies we have discussed in the previous sections. Now it is just a case of keeping going! As you can see from the gradual approach that we take to overcoming shyness or social anxiety, these problems are unlikely to go away overnight. It takes perseverance to keep working towards your child's ultimate goals. In our clinic we typically work with parents for a period of about two months. In that time we would expect noticeable changes, but we would not expect ultimate goals necessarily to have been reached. If they have, then there are often new goals to strive for. It is rarely the end of the work. Within that period of time, however, we find that families have normally had a good chance to put their new skills into practice and we often feel confident that they no longer need our help and can continue working on their goals as a family. From then on we encourage families to keep practising the skills they have learned, as this is the best way to maintain progress.

When progress is slow

At times it may feel as if you are not making progress, so then it is important to return to your early notes and compare how things are now with how they were when you started. You may be pleasantly surprised by the progress that has been made! However, if progress is nonetheless slow, you will need to make sure you have clear goals to focus on. In addition, of the different skills that we have described, it is likely that there are some that you have found worked particularly well with your child, while they may have taken to others less well. It will be useful to remember which strategies seemed to help your child most to use again when you want to make a concerted effort to help them face a particular fear in the future.

What has helped your child

In the following space, make a note of the strategies that you have found have particularly helped your child to overcome their social anxiety or shyness so that you can refer back to this. Once again, encourage your teenager to help you to fill this in or they may prefer to fill it in themselves (see Appendix 6 for records for teenagers).

Problems you may face

The box on page 198 describes some specific problems that parents have told us they have come across as they have tried to overcome their child's anxiety, including social anxiety. We urge you not to be put off by these problems, but to use the skills that you and your child have been practising with this book to surmount them. So (just as we have been encouraging you to do when helping your child), rather than telling you

Things I have done that have been helpful for reducing
my child's shyness/social anxiety

what to do we have suggested some strategies you might use to find your own solution. This way you are putting into practice the skills you have learned and also coming up with solutions that are going to suit you.

Common problems that parents face in overcoming their child's anxiety

Problem	Tips for finding a solution
Practical problems	
1 I don't have enough time to do the exercises.	How would it affect your time in the long term to put in the extra time now?
2 It's quicker (easier) just to do something for my child, rather than try to get them to do it themselves.	Is this really true when you think about it in the long term as well as the short term?
3 I don't know when to push my child. Are they anxious or are they not interested?	Is there a strategy that you could use whatever the reason (e.g. rewards)?
4 Other family members have different ideas about what is the right thing to do.	Could you share other chapters in this book with your family?
5 When my child 'acts up' I don't know if this is because they are upset or being difficult.	Again, is there a strategy that you could use whatever the reason (e.g. rewards)?
6 I'm not there at the times when my child gets anxious.	How can you encourage your child to use the strategies independently? Who else can you get involved?

7 It seems unfair to my other children to be rewarding one child for doing things they do all the time.	Is there anything your other children would benefit from being rewarded for?
8 We know what my child needs to do to overcome their fears, but those situations just don't happen very often in everyday life.	Think about creating the right opportunities.

Personal problems

1 I find it hard to keep motivated to keep 'pushing' my child.	See the section 'Managing your own anxiety'.
2 I can't help worrying about how my child will be able to manage if I give them a push.	What is it that worries you? Could there be another way of thinking about this?
3 It's hard to push my child to do something, when other members of the family have the same problem and aren't doing anything about it.	How can others in the family get involved?

One common problem that arises is when two parents have different approaches to the management of their child's anxious feelings and behaviors. This was the case for Peter's parents. They had separated many years ago and although Peter still saw his father regularly, his mum and dad did not get along very well. Peter's father felt that Peter's mother was making a big fuss about Peter's social anxiety and that Peter didn't really have a problem at all. This was perhaps partly due to Peter's dad being a bit shy so, like Peter, he didn't socialize very much. He thought Peter's behavior was normal and so didn't understand why Peter's mum had embarked on this program. This caused problems as Peter spent quite a bit of time with his dad but didn't practise anything he and his mum had planned while he was with him. Peter's dad also allowed Peter to avoid any social situation that made him feel nervous, which was the opposite of what Peter's mum was trying to do. It also meant Peter got cross with his mum and stepdad as he couldn't see why he had to try to confront his fears when his dad said he didn't have to. Peter's mum and stepdad used the problem-solving steps in Step 5 to see if they could come up with any solutions to this difficult situation (see opposite).

Keep practising

If things have been going well and your child has made great progress, then it will be tempting to stop practising the techniques and sit back and reap the rewards of your hard work! You must, however, keep on your toes and be on the lookout for opportunities to continue using the strategies. The more familiar your child is with the strategies, the more they will become your child's habitual way of dealing with problems and the better prepared your child will be to cope with any problems they face in the future and throughout their life.

As Peter's mum and stepdad were concerned about Peter's anxiety about attending parties, when he was able to go to a party they had got further than any of them had imagined.

Peter's mum and stepdad's problem-solving

What is the problem?	List all the possible solutions	What would happen if we chose this solution? In the short term? In the long term? To our anxiety in the future?	Is this plan doable? Yes/No	How good is this plan? Rate 0–10	What happened?
Peter's dad doesn't believe Peter has any social anxiety so lets him avoid all the situations he finds nerve-racking.	1 Carry on as we are. 2 Tell Peter's dad he must follow what we are doing or else Peter will get worse. 3 Get Paul (Peter's stepdad) to talk to Peter's dad and see if we can get him to read a bit of the book and some of our records. Paul could also show him what Peter's teacher has said about his anxiety.	1 Nothing would change. We would carry on trying and maybe make some progress, but it would be really slow and Peter would take a step back every time he went to his dad's. 2 He would think we were criticizing him, particularly me, as we don't get on well. We'd get into an argument and it would make things worse. 3 He might listen to Paul as they get on okay. He might read the book and the records and the teacher's report might help him to see that some-thing needs to be done.	Yes Yes Yes	3 1 7	Paul spoke to Peter's dad and they got on quite well. He read the stuff and did think the teacher might have a point. He has agreed to help with the step plan, which is great.

That did not stop them continuing to use their new skills however. There were lots of other things that Peter needed to work on, such as going to school and mixing with people he didn't know very well. Whenever any situation came up that worried Peter they continued to help him to think helpful thoughts, encouraged him to face his anxiety (rather than avoid it) or problem-solve to find a solution. As his life progressed he became a more confident and sociable individual.

Future goals

Have a think now about what you feel it is important for you and your child to continue to work on. Make a note of this in the following section so that you can refer back to it in the future to see whether you have begun to work towards those goals and what progress you have made. Your teenager may be able to help you with this or decide on their own goals for the future (see Appendix 6 for records for teenagers).

Michael met his ultimate goal of going to Beavers, but once he had achieved this it became clear to his parents that, because of his social anxiety, there were still certain things he would not do. For example, Michael's parents were keen for him to use the school toilets as he sometimes wet himself at school but Michael refused because he felt very nervous about it. He also didn't like answering questions in class. Michael's parents decided to generate a new list of goals to continue to work on.

Goals for my child and me to continue to work towards

1 _____

2 _____

3 _____

4 _____

5 _____

6 _____

7 _____

8 _____

9 _____

10 _____

Goals for us to work towards with Michael

1 Michael to answer questions in class _____

2 Michael to ask if he could join in _____
football/other games _____

3 Michael to go to a holiday club _____

4 Michael to use the school toilets regularly_____

Reward yourself!

Finally, we would like you to take this opportunity to stop and think about the achievements that you and your child have made. Throughout the program you will have been rewarding your child for their efforts and we hope that you will continue to do so. At this point, though, you should also acknowledge that if your child has made progress then it has been down to the help that you have been giving them. Although we are sure that your child's progress is a reward in itself, perhaps the time has come to reward yourself for all the work that you have put in to make this happen! Have a nice meal, arrange a night out, or get together with a friend. Whatever you do be sure to mark the occasion and give yourself the credit that you deserve for helping your child to overcome their shyness or social anxiety.

Lauren, with the help of her mum, managed to start asking the teacher for help although it was a bit of a struggle and Lauren slipped back a few times when she had a supply teacher or was feeling less confident. However, she did it and received her ultimate reward of having her bedroom decorated. Lauren and her mum started to work on another situation that Lauren found hard – reading aloud in class. Lauren's mum was quite exhausted with all the energy she had put in to helping Lauren, particularly as, being a single parent, she felt that she had no back-up from anyone. Although it had been hard work, she could now see the clear gains that Lauren had made as a result of her efforts and went out with her yoga friend for a nice meal to celebrate.

Keeping it going

Key points

- Keep practising the skills you have learned.
- Keep working towards new goals.
- Use these skills to overcome problems along the way.
- Reward yourself for the work you have done and the progress you have made. Well done!

PART THREE

Dealing with Further Problems

17

My child won't go to school

Why do children with social anxiety often find going to school hard?

Children who are socially anxious often have problems attending school because they expect other children or teachers to think badly of them or to be nasty to them and so understandably try to avoid it. For example, Peter often felt sick before school because he was anxious about going. He found it hard to mix with the other boys at school and worried that he would get picked on. Lauren also got anxious about school and often had a headache on the days that she had to sit a test. She worried that the teachers would think she was no good at her work, that she would do badly in tests, and she worried that everyone would think she was stupid if she asked for help in class. Sometimes children are anxious about going to school because they are being bullied. This is a very real problem and it is essential that children, and schools, find effective ways of dealing with it. We will talk about how to tackle this problem later in this chapter.

What should you do if your child refuses to go to school?

The first thing you need to do if your child either refuses to go to school or gets very anxious or nervous before school is to find out exactly what it is that is making them nervous. Just as you have practised in relation to other social anxieties, the first step is to ask your child simple questions to try to get a good understanding of their fear. Examples include: 'What worries you about going to school?' 'What do you think will happen if you do go to school?' or even, 'What is the worst thing that might happen if you do go to school?' Your child may be reluctant to tell you why they are worried. Peter didn't want to tell his mum about the teasing at school because he thought she would go up to school and sort it out. He was concerned that the other children would get told off and he would be accused of telling on them, which he thought would make the whole situation much worse. So, like Peter, your child may not tell you straight away what the problem is but it is worth persisting. Look back at Step 1 or other ideas on how to get your child to share their worries with you and for tips on how to do this with younger children.

If you are really unable to get information from your child about the source of their worries, it may be necessary to talk with your child's teacher or someone else who knows them well. It is important to be open with your child that you are doing this, but also to let them know that you are doing it as discreetly as possible so that it does not lead to increased anxiety.

Once you have established what your child is worried about, you need to make a plan of action in discussion with your child. If they have identified a particular problem that you both feel needs sorting out, use the strategies outlined in Step 5 to generate ways to solve the problem and evaluate them.

If you discover that there is not a particular problem at school but your child feels anxious about certain school activities or situations, such as answering questions in class or doing PE, take the opportunity to devise a step plan with your child to face their fear just as Lauren and her mother did (see Step 4). You can also encourage your child to challenge their anxious thoughts about these school situations by examining the evidence for and against their thoughts, testing out thoughts and considering alternatives (see Steps 1 and 2).

Getting support from your child's school

You may be concerned that your child's school is not going to look kindly on the fact that your child has been missing school. In today's climate there is so much press attention on parents being prosecuted for their children's failure to attend school that parents can feel persecuted and as if they and the school are on opposing sides. It is certainly the case that schools do worry about children who are not in school and sometimes involve an education welfare officer who is responsible for monitoring and encouraging a child's attendance. Legally, your child should be in school full-time. However, being anxious about school is an understandable reason why your child might be missing school. It is our experience that schools are generally very understanding and helpful if they can see that you are trying to get your child back into school, and they will appreciate your efforts to work with them to get your child back into school full-time.

Schools and education welfare services are familiar with the principle of children taking a step-by-step approach to returning to school. This must, of course, be negotiated with the school from the start so you will need to arrange a meeting with your child's teacher, head teacher or head of year and anyone else involved in monitoring and supporting your child's attendance. At this meeting discuss the possibility of working out a step-by-step plan with the school (take along a copy of Chapter 20 'Overcoming children's shyness and social anxiety: A brief guide for teachers' to show your child's teacher). If your child is currently not attending school, this may involve gradually building up the amount of time that they spend at school. It is important not to take for granted how hard this may be for your child, so concrete rewards should be worked out in advance and given as quickly as possible after your child meets their goal. Below is an example of the step-by-step plan that Peter, his mum and his school devised together.

Peter's step-by-step plan

1 Get dressed in my school uniform and go with my mum to take my little brother to school.
2 Go to school with Mum and talk to the teacher for ten minutes.
3 Go into school for one lesson but sit in the resource unit to do my work with one of my friends.
4 Go to the first lesson every day and if it gets too hard, go to the resource unit.
5 Go to the first lesson and break every day.

6 Go to school until lunchtime every day.
7 Go to school all day but come home for lunch.
8 Go to school and stay all day.

Ultimate goal: Go to school full-time for a week.

It is also useful to establish whether there is somewhere that your child can go to calm down and where they feel a bit safer so that they can withdraw from stress without having to leave the school grounds. A resource unit is an excellent place to go but not all schools have them. If your child's school doesn't have one, ask the teacher where else might be a good place for your child to go. It could simply be the head of year's office or the main office. Having a named person to go to if your child feels anxious can also be important. It will also be necessary to negotiate how your child gets access to this place or person, for example if they feel overwhelmed during a lesson and feel unable to express their concerns to the teacher or in front of the class. Schools sometimes give a child a card that they can present to the teacher which will allow them 'time out' to calm down at times of high anxiety. This enables your child to let the teacher know that they are feeling anxious without having to speak up in front of the class. If this strategy is used, it is essential that all your child's teachers are aware of it and have agreed to follow it.

Another good system is the use of buddies, where the school identifies an older pupil who your child can go to for support if they need it; this might be someone who arranges to meet up with your child each day to see how they are getting on.

The central message behind all this is that the aim should be to build up your child's attendance gradually with as many systems in place as possible to help them be comfortable staying in school for as long as has been set out on the step-by-step plan. You will achieve this most successfully if you work as a team with your child's school.

How to work as a team with your child's school

1 Arrange to speak to your child's teacher or head of year as soon as you notice that your child is regularly missing days at school.

2 Explain why you think your child is anxious about attending school and also ask for the teacher's opinion.

3 Raise any problems that your child has talked to you about at school, such as bullying, so that the school can deal with these.

4 Make a step plan to help your child to get back into school. Do this with both your child and their teacher, as they might also have some good ideas.

5 Talk about the possibility of having a safe place for your child to go, a teacher to go to, or a buddy.

6 Meet regularly with your child's teacher to review progress and iron out any problems with the step plan.

7 Be positive about your child's school even if you don't

think it has handled the situation very well. If you moan about your child's school, your child is even less likely to go back.

8 Be clear with your child that they have to go to school despite their anxieties but that you are there to support them in doing so. Not only does this give the message that avoiding the situation is not an option, but it also shows the school that you are serious about getting your child back to school.

Should I move my child to a different school?

Often parents who come to our clinic with children who are not attending school ask whether changing schools would be a good idea. Children are often very keen to move schools as they feel it will solve all their problems. They are likely to believe that they won't feel anxious at the new school and will make lots of friends. Unfortunately, changing schools rarely leads to a child becoming less anxious and usually the same problems occur, perhaps after a short 'honeymoon' period at the new school when everything goes well. As we have said, children who are highly anxious often find attending school hard because they have to answer questions in class, take tests, do work in small groups, mix with other children at playtime or cope with what other children might say to them. They will still have to do all these things in a new school.

On the other hand, if your child's fears about school relate to particular children being nasty to them, or not feeling that they have many friends, you may feel that moving school is a logical step. However, even in this situation, a school move may not solve all your child's problems. They may find initially at this new school that many people are nice to them and they may make some new friends, but if they have found making friends hard before, they may well find it hard again. Similarly, there is a good chance that there will be some children who can be unpleasant at the new school. If your child has poor social skills, or a lack of confidence in interacting with other people, this might make them more of a target for these children. What your child really needs to do is to learn how to make good friends and to learn how to deal with other children saying nasty things, together with support from the school.

There are occasionally times when moving schools might help to resolve your child's problems. If, for example, your child has some significant learning problems that can't be sufficiently supported in the current school, a school move might be a sensible option. However, this should only be considered after discussion with your child's teachers to see if there is anything that can be done to support your child better at their current school.

Changing schools is very unsettling for any child as they have to get used to new teachers, new children and a new school layout, and this can cause additional anxiety at first. If you are considering moving your child to a new school, you should think about this very carefully and talk to your child's teacher who might be able to give you some good advice.

What about home tuition?

Some children find going to school so hard that they just want to stay at home. They do not want to change schools as they know that going to another school will also make them feel nervous. Parents sometimes feel that it would be better to educate their child at home, as school is just too distressing for them. Lots of children, and parents, mention home tuition to us at our clinic, and want to know whether this is an option for them. Home tuition is designed for children who cannot go to school. Usually, this is because a child is physically ill, for example being unable to walk due to a debilitating illness, or undergoing treatment for an illness such as cancer. For these children, school is not always an option. Occasionally, children with a problem that is not physical, such as anxiety or depression, also receive home tuition because it is apparent that their anxiety or depression is so severe that they are not able to go to school. However, this situation is rare and in this case home tuition is only available for a short period of time and for insufficient hours to cover everything that your child would be learning at school.

Our concern for children who are being taught at home is that this is unlikely to make a child's social anxiety any better, and in fact it may well make it worse. Home tuition effectively allows a child to avoid almost all social situations, as they do not even need to leave the house! They also miss out on seeing friends. It is much better to try to devise a step plan to get your child back into school gradually rather than to allow them to stay at home all the time. If your child's anxiety about school is very high, then this plan needs to be extremely gradual. Very occasionally, home tuition is used as part of a step plan, for example if a child has already missed a large amount of school. Having home tuition several hours a week might form part of the first few steps of a plan. The next steps would involve either going to school part-time or having home tuition within the school grounds, to help your child to get used to the school environment again. However, in this case your child must clearly understand that home tuition is part of a short-term, time-limited plan.

What about bullying?

Bullying is something that needs to be tackled. It can involve name-calling, other unpleasant remarks or physical aggression, such as pushing, hitting or fighting. All schools are required to have an anti-bullying policy. This is basically a guide to how they will manage any incidents of bullying within the school. If your child is being bullied, you must talk to the school so that it can deal with it in accordance with their policy. It is important that your child feels that they have some control over what happens as a result of the bullying. Your child should be included in open discussions about how bullying will be handled and they must have the opportunity to discuss any concerns they have about this so that measures can be taken to resolve these issues.

The first step is to talk to your child's school so that it is made aware of the bullying and can take responsibility for dealing with it and looking after your child's best interests.

Ideally, you should have a discussion with or try to arrange a meeting with your child's teacher so that you, your child and your child's teacher can have an open discussion about what has happened. There should be a clear message to your child that bullying is not acceptable and that definite action will be taken. As we have talked about earlier in this chapter, you need to form a team with your child's school, so that you can work together to support your child in coping with this situation.

The second step is that, with your help, your child will benefit from making a clear plan of how they should respond to any further bullying incidents. Use the problem-solving strategies described in Step 5 to help your child to work out different ways of responding to bullying situations and evaluate which would be the most effective for them. Your child's teacher may also have some good ideas about how best to respond so talk to them about your child's plan of action. There are also a number of books listed in 'Useful books and contacts' that offer guidance to children on how to respond to bullying. These may well give you and your child more ideas about how to respond to further unwanted attention from other children.

In our experience, schools are keen to be made aware of any bullying and are generally able to resolve problems effectively. However, if you feel that your attempts to work with your child's school have not been successful, it would be worth reading through the steps we recommend again to ensure that you have followed our suggestions. You might also want to talk to your child's year head or another member of staff whom you have found helpful in the past. If all else fails, you should arrange a meeting with the headteacher of your child's school to discuss your concerns further.

Peter was teased by other children at school. There were three boys who often called Peter names, which he found upsetting and made him more anxious about attending school. Peter, his mum and his stepfather arranged a meeting with the school to talk about how both Peter and the school could deal with the name-calling. Peter's school outlined to Peter and his family how it intended to deal with the teasing. This included disciplining the three boys involved and providing Peter with more support in school. Peter was given permission to go to the resource unit at school whenever he was teased by the other children so that he could report the incident to the head of the unit and talk to her about how he responded to the boys. This also gave Peter the opportunity to sit in a quiet place and try to calm down using some relaxation techniques (see Chapter 19), as the name-calling made Peter very nervous. Peter and his parents also devised a plan of action for how he should respond to the teasing using the problem-solving techniques in Step 5 (see the table on the next page). Once Peter had decided on the best way to respond, he tried this out when the boys teased him, and talked to the head of the resource unit and his parents, once he got home, about how it went.

Problem-solving: Peter's example

What is the problem?	List all the possible solutions	What would happen if I chose this solution?	Is this plan doable? Yes/No	How good is this plan? Rate 0–10	What happened?
Boys at school calling me names.	1 Stay home.	I would get into trouble and so would Mum and Dad. I would get more anxious about going to school.	Not really	2	
	2 Call names back or hit them.	I would get into trouble and get a detention.	Yes	5	
	3 Tell them I don't like it and go and tell the teacher.	The boys might call me a grass but they would get told off and it might stop them.	Yes	7	I told Mrs King, the head of the resource unit, and she followed the plan that we had agreed.
	4 Ignore them.	I wouldn't get into trouble and they might stop it eventually but they might not.	Yes	6	

My child won't go to school

Key points

- Try to find out why your child is refusing to go to school by speaking to your child and key school personnel.
- Work as a team with your child's school.
- Devise a step plan to help your child to get back into school.
- Make sure your child's school tackles any bullying that your child reports.
- Work with your child to develop solutions to problem situations.

18

My child won't speak

Sometimes children who are perfectly able to speak do not speak when they are in public. These children are chatty at home among their family and, possibly, close friends, but in other places, like school, they are silent. This problem is often referred to as 'selective mutism' and is generally seen as a form of social anxiety. The methods we have used in this book are entirely appropriate for overcoming selective mutism and we will talk more in this chapter about how to implement them with your silent child. Below is an example of a boy with selective mutism.

Jonathan had always been a shy child and as his speech began to develop it became clear that he had some articulation problems that made it difficult for others to understand him. In time, his speaking became restricted to very familiar people only (his mum, dad and sister), despite the fact that his speech, when he did talk, had become much clearer.

Jonathan's parents were both shy themselves and found it really uncomfortable in social situations when someone spoke to Jonathan and he didn't respond. They started off by telling Jonathan to reply but he refused, which they found embarrassing. In the end, they just stopped going out with Jonathan as much as possible. At school Jonathan didn't talk at all. His teacher was worried about how well Jonathan would be able to learn and interact socially. She was also nervous of making the situation worse by pushing him to speak so she stopped asking him questions and hoped the day would come when he would feel able to join in.

Changing your child's thoughts about speaking

Children with selective mutism often worry that something bad will happen if they speak. These anxious thoughts lead them to avoid speaking unless they feel safe. The strategies we talked about earlier to tackle anxious thoughts (Steps 1 and 2) can be used to address your child's fears about speaking. If your child only speaks in a limited number of places you will not, of course, be able to address your child's anxious thoughts when you are in the feared situation as your child will not want to talk to you then. Instead try to discuss your child's thoughts when you are alone together as soon as possible after the event. Your child may find it hard to remember exactly what they were thinking at that time. If so, try to recreate the situation by describing what was happening in detail (with all the sights, sounds, smells!) or acting out the situation with your child.

Your child may feel silly or different for thinking the way they do, so be careful to listen to what they tell you and show that you are taking it seriously. You can then help your child to work out whether there is good cause for thinking the way they do, or whether there may be any other ways of thinking about this situation. The conversation that Jonathan and his dad had after they got back from visiting a relative is shown below.

Dad: Jonathan, earlier on when Auntie Jane offered you a biscuit you didn't answer her. Why was that? What did you think would happen if you did?

Jonathan: She would laugh at me.

Dad: What makes you think she'd laugh at you?

Jonathan: She would because she would think I sound funny when I speak and she wouldn't know what I said.

Dad: I see. That does sound like it might be scary for you. Has that happened before? Has Auntie Jane laughed at you before when you have spoken?

Jonathan: No, because I don't speak to her.

Dad: So because you haven't spoken to her I suppose you don't know if she'd laugh or not. Have other people laughed at you when you've spoken to them?

Jonathan: I only speak to you and Mum and Jessica [sister].

Dad: And have we laughed at how you speak?

Jonathan: No.

Dad: So it sounds like you're saying that you don't know if other people would laugh at you because you haven't spoken to anyone but us for so long. But we don't laugh at you so maybe other people wouldn't either? If you had answered Auntie Jane what would you have said?

Jonathan: I would have said, 'Yes, please.'

Dad: So one thing that might have happened would have been her laughing at you. What else could have happened?

Jonathan: She might have given me a biscuit.

Dad: That's true – she might have done. So how can we find out what would happen?

Speaking up leads to good things happening

Giving your child positive feedback is important if you are to help them to start to speak in public. In particular it is essential to be on the lookout for any time when your child does speak or communicate (even non-verbally) with someone outside the close family and praise or reward this. Parents often fear that by praising or rewarding their child's attempts at speaking they may be 'making a big deal out of it', which might put their child off doing it again. The important thing will be *how* you give your praise. Of course, if your child is very anxious about what other people think of them and when they do speak up, you say loudly in front of a room of strangers, 'Wow. Well done, Bobby. You *never* normally say anything when we are out of the house. Well done!', they may well find this embarrassing! In this situation a simple acknowledgement of what they have done (a little pat on the back, wink of the eye, or quiet 'Well done') will let them know you have noticed and appreciated what they have done. Then when you are back in a 'safe' place you can give the clear and specific praise that we discussed earlier.

Speaking up yourself

Earlier we also talked about the importance of what your child sees you do and how you respond to different situations (Part Two, Additional principles 2). Try to take opportunities to talk to people outside your immediate family and friendships; for example, rather than just handing over the money at the cash till say a few words. You don't need to go overboard, but a relaxed 'Hello' with a smile is a good start.

Having a go at speaking up

Your child now needs to have a go at speaking up to discover for themselves that it may not necessarily lead to bad things happening; you can use a step-by-step plan to devise a plan of action (Step 4). The early steps may not actually be speaking but may be communicating in some other, non-verbal way. For example, putting a hand up or making a different, non-verbal sound. Below is Jonathan's step-by-step plan.

STEP 1   Look up at the teacher when she calls my name for the register

Helpful Thought: *I have looked at my teacher once or twice before. Nothing bad has happened when I've done it, and I'll get a sticker if I do it this time.*

Reward: *Sticker from the teacher. Praise from Mum and Dad.*

STEP 2   Raise my hand when the teacher calls my name for the register

Helpful Thought:
Reward: *Sticker from the teacher. Praise from Mum and Dad.*

STEP 3   Say 'here Miss', on the phone to the teacher
Helpful Thought:
Reward: *Dad will play computer game with me for 20 minutes.*

STEP 4   Say 'here Miss' to the teacher before the others arrive for class
Helpful Thought:
Reward: *Sticker from the teacher. Special trip to the park after school.*

STEP 5   Say 'here Miss' to the teacher with one other child in the room (Joshua)
Helpful Thought:
Reward: *Sticker from the teacher. Trip to the pound shop with £1 to spend after school.*

STEP 6   Say 'here Miss' to the teacher in a small group (Learning Support Group)
Helpful Thought:
Reward: *Sticker from the teacher. Swimming.*

ULTIMATE GOAL: Answer 'here Miss' to the register in front of the class
Helpful Thought:
Reward: *Sticker from the teacher. Dinner out with the whole family at Jonathan's favourite restaurant.*

Jonathan not answering the register was only one situation that his parents were concerned about. When he had achieved this goal, together the family devised a new step-by-step plan for another of Jonathan's anxieties about speaking, talking to the lady at the local shop.

Creating opportunities for speaking

In the same way as we have encouraged you to engage your child in a variety of social activities (Part Two, Additional principles 1), it is important, with a silent child, to create regular opportunities for your child to speak to people, even if, in the event, they do not do so. For example, go together to shops, the library, perhaps go on the bus or train, even enrol your child in a club where they will have lots of speaking opportunities (this may require some planning such as talking to the club leader in advance to make sure your child can participate even if they are unable to speak).

Form a team with your child's teacher

As you can see above, Jonathan's teacher was very involved in his step-by-step plan. If a child is not speaking in school then working together with your child's school staff is essential (Chapter 20, 'Overcoming children's shyness and social anxiety: A brief guide for teachers', will provide your child's teacher with an overview of the strategies that we outline in this book).

Your child is likely to find it difficult to draw up a step-by-step plan with you and their teacher present, so arrange a meeting with your child's teacher before you work on the step plan to make sure you know what the teacher will be willing to do within (and outside) lessons. Is there an existing reward/sticker system in the class for behavior or achievements? Will the teacher give your child rewards for reaching specific goals? Will the teacher be able to help to create certain situations, even though they might not be part of the normal school day (e.g. meeting Jonathan before class to have a practice run)? Or perhaps other situations already exist that can be used within the step plan (e.g. Jonathan already worked in a group with two other children for learning support)?

Teachers have different commitments and so their ability, for example, to spend time out of lessons working with your child on their step plan cannot be taken for granted. It will be important to know what your child's teacher will be able to do and also whether there are other staff (e.g. Learning Support Assistants) who may be able to contribute to the plan.

Different teachers will also have different views on using rewards in class. If your child's teacher does have reservations about using rewards we would encourage you to share the section on this from Chapter 5 with them. We have been particularly impressed with the results of having a whole class reward system, in which all members of the class can earn rewards (e.g. stickers) for behaviors that the teacher recognizes as being an achievement for the particular child, but which contribute to the total for the whole class. This way the whole class support each individual's achievement and they will all be behind your child's progress.

Once you know what will be possible within your child's school you can work out a step-by-step plan with your child (see Chapter 17, 'My child won't go to school', for an example of how Peter's parents worked as a team with his school). You will need then to share this with the teacher and make sure they are in agreement. It will also be essential to have a system for keeping in touch with your child's teacher to monitor your child's progress, so that you can make sure they get their rewards straight away. This may all seem like a lot for both you and your child's teacher to take on, but it is vital for your child to overcome a fear of speaking in school, and will be well worth it in the end.

Social skills and problem-solving

Children with selective mutism are also likely to have poor social skills or lack confidence in mixing with others as they rarely have the opportunity to practise these skills due to their reluctance to speak. For this reason, once your child has started to speak a little, it is important that you try to help them to improve their social skills (see Part Two, Additional principles 1). Similarly, problem-solving skills will be helpful for you and your child in a range of problem situations that might arise (see Part Two, Step 5).

My child won't speak

Key points

- Selective mutism describes a condition when children who can speak do not speak in particular social situations.
- Selective mutism is a form of social anxiety.
- All the methods in this book are appropriate for overcoming selective mutism.
- If your child is not speaking in school, it will be essential to form a team with your child's school to overcome this.

19

Relaxation

Who should learn relaxation techniques?

In Part One, we talked about the physical symptoms of anxiety that your child may experience. These included tummy aches or headaches, breathing more quickly and sweaty hands or dizziness. In our clinic we do not generally tackle these unpleasant physical symptoms of anxiety in their own right, as we tend to find that reducing fear by changing how a shy or socially anxious child thinks and how they behave has a knock-on effect on these unpleasant sensations. Sometimes, however, the physical symptoms that a child experiences cause a great deal of distress and the child needs to learn that (a) these physical symptoms are not harmful and (b) that they can take control of them. The strategies throughout Part Two will help you to find ways to investigate with your child the view that these symptoms are harmful (e.g. by looking into the evidence and carrying out experiments). This chapter describes ways in which your child can also learn to take control of these physical symptoms. Relaxation techniques are appropriate for children of all ages. However, as before, young children will need a considerable amount of guidance from you while teenagers will be able to learn these techniques independently.

What do relaxation techniques do?

Relaxation techniques do three things. The first is to reduce muscle tension. We know that when people become anxious their muscles become tight. As we described in Part One, this indicates that your child's body is preparing to take action because their brain has given their body the message that there is danger around. Muscle tension is an unpleasant feeling and may result in headaches or other physical signs of anxiety. The second thing that relaxation techniques do is to help us to control our breathing. When we are anxious, we breathe more quickly and less deeply, so less oxygen enters our bodies. This leads to various physical sensations such as your child feeling as if they cannot breathe or having butterflies in their stomach. The third role of relaxation is to give your child a sense of control over their anxieties by taking action.

How does your child learn to relax?

To achieve relaxation can take a lot of practice. We recommend that children practise the strategies described in this chapter every day at the same time, until they get really good at them. Your child will need your help to do them initially and so it is best if you do them together. However, your teenager may be reluctant to do the exercises with you and, in any case, they are likely to be able to learn these techniques independently by reading the instructions on the following pages. Often a good time to practise relaxation techniques is before bed, as part of your child's bedtime routine. This may have the added bonus of helping them to settle to sleep better!

Different types of relaxation techniques

Most relaxation techniques aim to reduce muscle tension, control breathing or create calming mental imagery. However, there are various ways of doing this and so there are a number of different relaxation strategies available. Some relaxation techniques are very quick and only take a few minutes, while others take up to half an hour to complete. In principle, it is better to take longer to relax as it is likely to work better, particularly to start with. As your child gets more skilled at relaxing, they can cut down the amount of time they spend on the relaxation strategies.

Here we will describe three different relaxation techniques that can be used independently or in combination.

1 Muscle tension and relaxation

Progressive muscle relaxation teaches your child to relax their muscles, focusing on one group of muscles at a time. To do these exercises, your child needs to find somewhere comfortable and quiet to sit or lie down. As we have said, for pre-school and primary school-aged children, it is probably best if you do the exercises together, at least at first. Try to find a time when neither of you will be disturbed.

This process involves getting your child to tense and relax all their muscle groups, one after the other. You may be wondering why we are getting your child to tense their muscles when this is the very thing we are trying to reduce! However, relaxing muscles is an abstract concept and not very easy to do. It is much easier to get children first to tense muscles, then relax them, as they can clearly feel the difference between their muscles when they are tense and tight and when they are relaxed. As you go though the exercises with your child, you can ask them at different points, 'Does that feel tight?', 'Does that muscle feel different now you have relaxed it?', 'Can you notice the difference?' They should tense their muscles so that they feel tight but are not painful. For each muscle group, they should tense the muscles for 3 seconds (count to 3 slowly) and then relax the muscles for 3 seconds (count to 3 slowly) using the guidelines below. The relaxing bit is most important, so they can relax the muscles for a bit longer if they like.

Muscle Relaxation

Hands: Clench each fist (one at a time) for 3 seconds and then relax each hand for 3 seconds.

Arms: Bend each elbow so the wrist nearly touches the shoulder (one at a time) and hold for 3 seconds, then relax each arm for a further 3 seconds.

Legs: Point the toes and straighten the leg, pushing the knee down, so both the calf and thigh muscles tighten for 3 seconds, then relax this leg for 3 seconds. Repeat with the other leg.

Bottom: Squeeze the bottom as if trying to lift it off the bed or chair for 3 seconds, then relax it for 3 seconds.

Stomach: Pull in the stomach and hold for 3 seconds, then relax it for 3 seconds.

Chest: Stick out the chest like a bodybuilder and take a deep breath in, hold it for 3 seconds then relax for a further 3 seconds.

Shoulders and neck: Pull the shoulders up to the ears (or as close as they can get), and hold for 3 seconds, then relax for a further 3 seconds.

Mouth: Clench the teeth and do a big wide smile and hold for 3 seconds, then relax the mouth completely for 3 seconds.

Eyes: Scrunch up the eyes so they are tightly shut for 3 seconds, then relax the eyes, but keep them shut for at least 3 seconds.

Forehead: Put a hand on the head to make sure it does not move! Raise the eyes to look at the ceiling so the forehead becomes wrinkled. Hold for 3 seconds and relax for 3 seconds.

These exercises should take about 5–10 minutes. If you find your child is doing them more quickly, slow things down by having a bigger gap between each exercise, and by relaxing for longer than 3 seconds after each muscle group has been tightened.

2 Breathing

Your child needs to learn to breathe both slowly and deeply in order to relax properly. If their breathing is very shallow, this is likely to make them feel more anxious.

First of all, show your child how to breathe in through their nose and out through their mouth. Second, your child should count to three slowly in their head when they are breathing in, and count to four slowly when they are breathing out, so that they breathe out for a bit longer than they breathe in. By counting, your child is automatically slowing down their breathing, which we know can get quicker when they are anxious. Finally, you need to make sure your child is breathing nice and deeply. You can tell if they are by seeing if their chest moves up and down as they breathe in and out. If it does, they are breathing quite deeply, but encourage them to breathe even more deeply by taking deeper breaths in and out. If their chest hardly moves then their breathing is quite shallow and they need to work on breathing more deeply as this will get more oxygen into their body.

When your child has practised this type of breathing they can use it between tensing and relaxing exercises, rather than doing it afterwards. For example, they can tense and relax the hands, then do some slow deep breathing, followed by tensing and relaxing the arms, and so on. When your child gets really good at deep slow breathing, they could say 'relax' to themselves as they breathe out, rather than counting, so that they begin to associate the word 'relax' with this relaxed state.

Slow deep breathing is also great if your child feels anxious when they are out and do not want to do the tensing and relaxing exercises in front of others. People rarely notice how other people breathe so they could do this without drawing any attention to themselves.

3 Imagery

Another powerful way to relax is by using mental imagery techniques – in other words helping your child to create a relaxing scene in their mind. There are lots of different techniques you can use; some take a few minutes, some a lot longer. This is the area where you and your child can be most creative.

One of the best strategies is to get your child to close their eyes and think of a favourite place, somewhere that makes them feel calm, happy and relaxed. This works best if the child chooses the place where they want to 'go' to for themselves. It could be a favourite beach from a holiday, the football stadium of a favourite team, your child's bedroom or an imaginary place they have never been to. Your job is to act as the guide by asking questions to help them to recreate the sights and sounds and smells of that place. Encourage your child to tell you about these things in as much detail as possible. For example, can they hear the sea, or the birds, or even the wind? Can they smell the salt of the sea? Can they hear the crowd cheering, music playing or smell the hot dogs? Allow your child to enjoy this image for as long as they are comfortable then gently ask them to open their eyes without losing that relaxed sensation.

When should my child use these exercises?

As we have said, relaxation techniques are a skill that needs to be learned and practised over and over again. Your child is unlikely to find them easy. Practise the strategies that we have outlined above with your child every day until you notice that they are able to relax more and more easily.

It is a good idea to continue doing them every day even when your child has got really good at them so that this skill is not lost. Your child will then find it easier to use these techniques at times when they actually feel anxious, for example in the morning before an important test.

A word of warning

Some children find relaxation exercises quite boring and they are not terribly keen to do them. If this is how your child responds to your attempts to help them to relax, they will not be the only one! You therefore need to try to make these exercises as fun as possible. For example, the difference between tension and relaxation can be demonstrated by pretending to be two different characters that your child is interested in: one who is very stiff and another who is very floppy. This particularly helps younger children who find relaxation exercises difficult to grasp. Some examples are given below.

Stiff examples	Floppy examples
A robot	A rag-doll
A breadstick	A jelly
A cat about to pounce	A cat asleep on the bed

For the breathing exercises try challenging your child to breathe as quietly as they possibly can – this breathing is likely to be slow and deep, just what you are trying to encourage.

Finally, for mental imagery the key point is that the scene that your child is creating is one that they have chosen, even if you think it is a very strange choice for a place to relax (e.g. a noisy football stadium). Teenagers often find relaxation techniques useful, but remember, as we said earlier, to allow your teenager to learn the strategies independently unless they specifically ask for your help.

Everyday activities

If, however, despite valiant attempts to interest your child in relaxation exercises they are not interested, all is not lost because some everyday activities can be an extremely effective form of relaxation.

True relaxation describes a state in which we are not thinking about what has happened in the past or is going to happen in the future, but we are in a state of calm in the here and now. Simply engaging in an activity that is enjoyable and takes their full concentration will help your child to relax. This could be anything from watching an engrossing film, to playing sport, cooking or doing crafts. Exercise can be a particularly good form of relaxation. It can also help to lift people's mood and improve sleep. Exercise can be something as simple as walking the dog or strolling to the local shops. The most important thing is that the activity must be something that your child really enjoys and is not a source of additional anxiety. Once you have identified what sort of activities allow your child to relax make sure you build them in to their weekly routine so that your child gets a regular break from fears and worries.

Relaxation

Key points

- Relaxation techniques are particularly good for children who experience lots of physical symptoms of anxiety.
- Find ways of explaining relaxation exercises that fit with your child's interests.
- Get your child to practise the relaxation exercises regularly.
- Build enjoyable activities and exercise into your child's routine.

20

Overcoming children's shyness and social anxiety: A brief guide for teachers

We have written this chapter for teachers of shy and socially anxious children. It forms part of a book (*Overcoming your child's shyness and social anxiety: a self-help guide using cognitive-behavioral techniques* by Lucy Willetts and Cathy Creswell) that we have written for parents of shy and socially anxious children. We hope that it will provide you with a helpful summary of the techniques that we have outlined in the book so that you can use the same strategies in school as parents are using at home. Having read this chapter, if you would like more information about the strategies we have outlined, we suggest that you read the remainder of this book, in particular the guide in Part Two.

What are shyness and social anxiety?

Children who are shy feel nervous in more social situations, such as asking for help, going to a friend's for tea or talking to adults. They interact less with their classmates and can also be less assertive than children who are not shy. Social anxiety is extreme shyness. It is a specific form of anxiety in which children worry that they might do something stupid or embarrassing in these situations, such as saying something stupid, which will result in other children or adults laughing at them or thinking negatively about them. Children who experience social anxiety will try to avoid situations where there are other adults or children in order to avoid any embarrassment or discomfort and may experience physical symptoms of anxiety such as breathing quickly, butterflies in their stomach or sweaty hands.

Anxiety problems, including social anxiety, are actually the most commonly reported problems among children and teenagers. Children often do not grow out of these problems, and they can be a risk factor for other problems later in life. It is clearly essential that young people experiencing problems with social anxiety are supported in overcoming these difficulties.

Shyness and social anxiety in school

Social anxiety problems often underlie difficulties at school and can prevent children from reaching their true potential. Children who experience anxiety about social situations often have difficulties with attendance as they try hard to avoid a range of social situations, many of which occur in school. Shy and socially anxious children also find numerous situations within school difficult, including asking for help, speaking up in class, mixing with peers, talking to teachers, doing a presentation or participating in PE.

What can be done?

There are various things that can be done in school to help children to overcome their shyness or social anxiety alongside parents or carers implementing similar strategies at home. Below we outline strategies that teachers or other school staff can use with children to help them to overcome their shyness or social anxiety.

Overcoming shyness and social anxiety in school

The central characteristics of shyness and social anxiety are:

1   A tendency to notice possible threat and danger easily. Shy and socially anxious children think that other people will think of them in a negative way.

2   A tendency to feel out of control in the face of possible danger or threat. Shy and socially anxious children worry that they will not cope when they are in social situations and may embarrass themselves.

3   A tendency to avoid facing possible threat or danger. Shy and socially anxious children try to avoid social situations that make them nervous or scared. This is particularly true for children with social anxiety.

The trouble is that if a child always avoids social situations where they see possible danger or threat then they (a) never get the opportunity to see that in fact the danger may not actually exist (i.e. that other people might not think of them in a negative way), and (b) never get the opportunity to learn the skills to deal with potentially difficult situations.

Here's an example:

> *Jane thinks that if she answers a question in class she will get it wrong and her classmates will think that she is stupid. When her teacher asks her a question, therefore, she looks down at her desk and doesn't answer. She doesn't ever get to find out whether in fact she did know the right answer, and if she didn't whether her classmates would even care.*

In helping a child to overcome shyness and social anxiety, therefore, the child needs to be supported in testing out their assumptions in order to discover that:

1 Things may not turn out as badly as they fear.
2 Even if things don't go well, there is likely to be something they can do about it.
3 By facing fears they can be overcome.

In practice

When a child is very shy or socially anxious and appears likely to become distressed a natural reaction from people around them is to try to minimize this as much as possible. For example:

> *Whenever Jane's teacher asked her a question she went red, avoided his eye contact and stared at the desk. This seemed just to attract more attention to Jane, which the teacher could see was not helping. Gradually the teacher stopped asking Jane questions and hoped that she would come to put her hand up more as time went on.*

Although the teacher's reaction in this example is completely understandable, in fact it served to reinforce Jane's avoidance of answering questions. Instead, we want to create opportunities for Jane to have a go at increasingly socially anxiety-provoking tasks and reward her attempts at these in order to help her to discover gradually that she can cope. Here is an example of what Jane's teacher did:

Jane's teacher sat down with Jane during break-time and let Jane know that he could see she was finding it hard to answer questions. He asked Jane what made it so difficult for her. Jane told him that she was worried that she might get the answer wrong. Jane's teacher suggested they set up an experiment to find out if she would get it wrong. Every day at break-time he would ask Jane one question from the lesson and they would see how many she got right. Having done this for a week, Jane and her teacher found that although she didn't always get the answer right she didn't get it wrong more than other people in the class would have done. Her teacher congratulated her. They then decided that, as she was so good at answering questions at break-time, it was now time to try answering questions when she was in a small group. He agreed that each day when she was working in a small group he would ask her a question about the work. Jane was worried that she would be singled out so he agreed he would also ask other children questions. Gradually, in this way, Jane and her teacher progressed from answering a question individually, to a small group, to the whole class and finally to asking the teacher a question herself.

Real threat

It is essential to identify whether the child's shyness or social anxiety is based on reality, rather than a misperception of the world around them. For example, if a child fears being bullied because they are being bullied, or fears making a mistake because they are struggling to keep up with the rest of the class academically, then these problems need to be rectified first of all. It is essential that the child see that where problems exist there are solutions to them.

Tips for helping children to overcome shyness and social anxiety in school

In helping children to test out and gradually face their fears the following tips can be useful:

- As much as possible work with the child to develop the gradual plan, encouraging the child to set goals.
- Be open and explicit with parents about the strategies you are using so that you can work together. If a similar approach is being taken at home and at school change will occur faster.
- Find ways to motivate and reward the child, including praise and tangible rewards (depending on age; stickers, being given responsibilities, e.g. the opportunity to make choices about class activities).
- Be positive – just having a go is an achievement in itself.
- If the child cannot achieve the goal then nothing bad should happen (as this would put the child off even

attempting it next time); the result is simply that the reward is not achieved.

- If a child struggles then the goal may be too difficult. Break it down into smaller steps.
- Be prepared for setbacks, they always happen. Just try again later or the next day.

Common concerns

The following are some common concerns raised by teachers and our responses to them.

- 'If I praise the child for this won't it just draw more attention to them?'
  All children are encouraged by praise, although it is true that some children find it uncomfortable to receive. In this situation it is not a question of whether to give it, but a question of how it is given. Just as other feared events are built up slowly, so can this. Negotiate with the child how they would like you to show that you are pleased with them. For example, it can start with a pat on the back as the child leaves the room or a wink of the eye – so long as the child knows that you have noticed their attempt to face the fear and you appreciate it.
- 'I don't want to bribe the children in my class by giving rewards.'
  In contrast to a bribe, rewards are there to help children to achieve goals that are going to benefit them (not you) in the long term. Children can't always see that doing something that is difficult may in fact be a good thing and so may need more immediate incentives

to encourage them to have a go. The reward also says to the child: 'I appreciate that you found that difficult but you still had a go. Well done!'

- 'I can hardly give rewards to one child in the class when all the other children just answer questions with no problem at all.'

  Would it be possible to start up a whole class system of rewards? All children have something that they find difficult to do (be it academic, social, emotional or behavioral) and for which encouragement would be beneficial. In fact having a reward system in which each member can earn rewards on behalf of the whole class encourages pupils to support each other in their different endeavours. Once a certain point has been reached (stickers on a chart, marbles in a jar, etc.) the whole class can receive a group reward (e.g. playing a game, choosing an activity).

- 'How am I supposed to find the time to do this?'

  The strategies described here have all been successfully used by teachers or other school personnel whom we have worked with. It is true that some extra time and thought may be required to get the ball rolling but often things can start to change quickly. We would hope that this work now will prevent a greater input of time further down the line, should problems become more entrenched. If, however, it is completely impractical for you to take this on, do you have a colleague who could do so (e.g. a teacher, an LSA, the head of year)?

APPENDICES

Appendix 1

Helping my child with 'unhelpful thoughts'

What is happening?	What are they thinking?	Evidence and alternatives	What happened in the end?
	Why are you worried?	What makes you think that ____ will happen?	What did your child think?
	What do you think will happen?	Has that ever happened to you before?	What did your child do?
	What is it about (this situation) that is making you worried?	Have you ever seen that happen to someone else?	How did your child feel?
		How likely is it that ____ will happen?	

Can you imagine that anything else could happen?

If ___ did happen, could there be any other reasons for it?

What would you think was happening if someone else was in the same boat?

What would (another child) think if they were in this situation?

How could you test out this thought?

Helping my child with 'unhelpful thoughts'

What is happening?	What are they thinking?	Evidence and alternatives	What happened in the end?
	Why are you worried?	What makes you think that _____ will happen?	What did your child think?
	What do you think will happen?	Has that ever happened to you before?	What did your child do?
	What is it about (this situation) that is making you worried?	Have you ever seen that happen to someone else?	How did your child feel?
		How likely is it that _____ will happen?	

Appendix 1

Can you imagine that anything else could happen?

If ____ did happen, could there be any other reasons for it?

What would you think was happening if someone else was in the same boat?

What would (another child) think if they were in this situation?

How could you test out this thought?

Appendix 1

Helping my child with 'unhelpful thoughts'

What is happening?	What are they thinking?	Evidence and alternatives	What happened in the end?
	Why are you worried?	What makes you think that ____ will happen?	What did your child think?
	What do you think will happen?	Has that ever happened to you before?	What did your child do?
	What is it about (this situation) that is making you worried?	Have you ever seen that happen to someone else?	How did your child feel?
		How likely is it that ____ will happen?	

Can you imagine that anything else could happen?

If ___ did happen, could there be any other reasons for it?

What would you think was happening if someone else was in the same boat?

What would (another child) think if they were in this situation?

How could you test out this thought?

Appendix 2

Responding to my child's shy or socially anxious behavior

Date	Behavior What did my child do?	Response What did I do?	Yes	No	Outcome What happened when I did this?
		Cut out reassurance. Asked about anxious thoughts. Helped my child find alternative thoughts. Gave clear and specific praise. Offered a reward. Showed how I managed my own fears about the situation. Overcame my worries about my child in this situation. Stood back and allowed my child to have a go.			
		Cut out reassurance. Asked about anxious thoughts. Helped my child find alternative thoughts. Gave clear and specific praise. Offered a reward. Showed how I managed my own fears about the situation. Overcame my worries about my child in this situation. Stood back and allowed my child to have a go.			

Cut out reassurance. Asked about anxious thoughts. Helped my child find alternative thoughts. Gave clear and specific praise. Offered a reward. Showed how I managed my own fears about the situation Overcame my worries about my child in this situation. Stood back and allowed my child to have a go.	
Cut out reassurance. Asked about anxious thoughts. Helped my child find alternative thoughts. Gave clear and specific praise. Offered a reward. Showed how I managed my own fears about the situation. Overcame my worries about my child in this situation. Stood back and allowed my child to have a go.	

Responding to my child's shy or socially anxious behavior

Date	Behavior What did my child do?	Response What did I do?	Yes	No	Outcome What happened when I did this?
		Cut out reassurance. Asked about anxious thoughts. Helped my child find alternative thoughts. Gave clear and specific praise. Offered a reward. Showed how I managed my own fears about the situation. Overcame my worries about my child in this situation. Stood back and allowed my child to have a go.			
		Cut out reassurance. Asked about anxious thoughts. Helped my child find alternative thoughts. Gave clear and specific praise. Offered a reward. Showed how I managed my own fears about the situation. Overcame my worries about my child in this situation. Stood back and allowed my child to have a go.			

Cut out reassurance. Asked about anxious thoughts. Helped my child find alternative thoughts. Gave clear and specific praise. Offered a reward. Showed how I managed my own fears about the situation Overcame my worries about my child in this situation. Stood back and allowed my child to have a go.	Cut out reassurance. Asked about anxious thoughts. Helped my child find alternative thoughts. Gave clear and specific praise. Offered a reward. Showed how I managed my own fears about the situation. Overcame my worries about my child in this situation. Stood back and allowed my child to have a go.

		Responding to my child's shy or socially anxious behavior			
Date	Behavior What did my child do?	Response What did I do?	Yes	No	Outcome What happened when I did this?
		Cut out reassurance. Asked about anxious thoughts. Helped my child find alternative thoughts. Gave clear and specific praise. Offered a reward. Showed how I managed my own fears about the situation. Overcame my worries about my child in this situation. Stood back and allowed my child to have a go.			
		Cut out reassurance. Asked about anxious thoughts. Helped my child find alternative thoughts. Gave clear and specific praise. Offered a reward. Showed how I managed my own fears about the situation. Overcame my worries about my child in this situation. Stood back and allowed my child to have a go.			

Cut out reassurance.	Cut out reassurance.
Asked about anxious thoughts.	Asked about anxious thoughts.
Helped my child find alternative thoughts.	Helped my child find alternative thoughts.
Gave clear and specific praise.	Gave clear and specific praise.
Offered a reward.	Offered a reward.
Showed how I managed my own fears about the situation	Showed how I managed my own fears about the situation.
Overcame my worries about my child in this situation.	Overcame my worries about my child in this situation.
Stood back and allowed my child to have a go.	Stood back and allowed my child to have a go.

Appendix 3

My child's step–by–step plan

Goal	Helpful Thought	Reward
1 (EASIEST STEP)		
2		
3		
4		
5		
6		
7		
8		
9		
10 (ULTIMATE GOAL)		

Appendix 3

My child's step-by-step plan

Goal	Helpful Thought	Reward
1 (EASIEST STEP)		
2		
3		
4		
5		
6		
7		
8		
9		
10 (ULTIMATE GOAL)		

Appendix 4

Problem-solving

What is the problem?	List all the possible solutions No matter how weird or wonderful	What would happen if I chose this solution? In the short term? In the long term? To my anxiety in the future?	Is this plan doable? Yes/No	How good is this plan? Rate 0–10	What happened?
	.				

Appendix 4

Problem-solving

What is the problem?	List all the possible solutions No matter how weird or wonderful	What would happen if I chose this solution? In the short term? In the long term? To my anxiety in the future?	Is this plan doable? Yes/No	How good is this plan? Rate 0–10	What happened?
	.				

Appendix 4

Appendix 4

Problem-solving

What is the problem?	List all the possible solutions No matter how weird or wonderful	What would happen if I chose this solution? In the short term? In the long term? To my anxiety in the future?	Is this plan doable? Yes/No	How good is this plan? Rate 0–10	What happened?

Appendix 4

Appendix 5

Helping myself with 'unhelpful thoughts'

What is happening?	What am I thinking?	Evidence and alternatives	What happened in the end?
	Why am I worried?	What makes me think that ____ will happen?	What did I think?
	What do I think will happen?	Has that ever happened to me before?	What did I do?
	What is it about (this situation) that is making me worried?	Have I ever seen that happen to someone else?	How did I feel?
		How likely is it that ____ will happen?	

Can I imagine that anything else
could happen?

If ____ did happen, could there be
any other reasons for it?

What would I think was happening if
someone else was in the same boat?

What would someone else think if
they were in this situation?

How could I test this out?

Appendix 5

Helping myself with 'unhelpful thoughts'

What is happening?	What am I thinking?	Evidence and alternatives	What happened in the end?
	Why am I worried?	What makes me think that _____ will happen?	What did I think?
	What do I think will happen?	Has that ever happened to me before?	What did I do?
	What is it about (this situation) that is making me worried?	Have I ever seen that happen to someone else?	How did I feel?
		How likely is it that _____ will happen?	

Can I imagine that anything else could happen?

If _____ did happen, could there be any other reasons for it?

What would I think was happening if someone else was in the same boat?

What would someone else think if they were in this situation?

How could I test this out?

Appendix 6

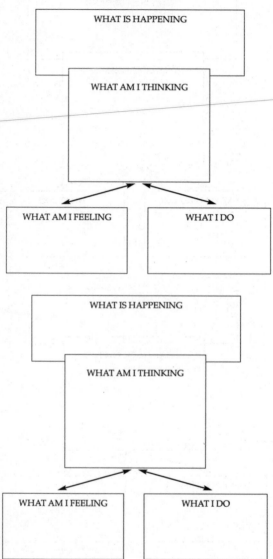

Appendix 6

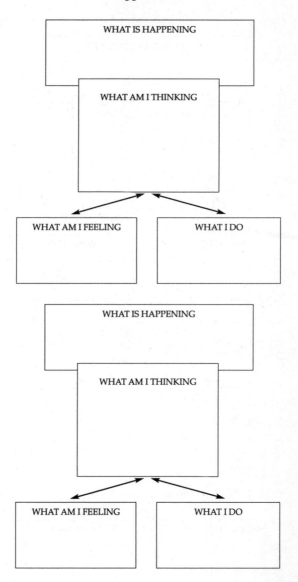

	Records for teenagers: Helping myself with 'unhelpful thoughts'		
What is happening?	**What am I thinking?**	**Evidence and alternatives**	**What happened in the end?**
	Why am I worried?	What makes me think that _____ will happen?	What did I think?
	What do I think will happen?	Has that ever happened to me before?	What did I do?
	What is it about (this situation) that is making me worried?	Have I ever seen that happen to someone else?	How did I feel?
		How likely is it that _____ will happen?	

Can I imagine that anything else could happen?

If _____ did happen, could there be any other reasons for it?

What would I think was happening if someone else was in the same boat?

What would someone else think if they were in this situation?

How could I test this out?

Records for teenagers: Helping myself with 'unhelpful thoughts'

What is happening?	What am I thinking?	Evidence and alternatives	What happened in the end?
	Why am I worried?	What makes me think that _____ will happen?	What did I think?
	What do I think will happen?	Has that ever happened to me before?	What did I do?
	What is it about (this situation) that is making me worried?	Have I ever seen that happen to someone else?	How did I feel?
		How likely is it that _____ will happen?	

Can I imagine that anything else could happen?

If _____ did happen, could there be any other reasons for it?

What would I think was happening if someone else was in the same boat?

What would someone else think if they were in this situation?

How could I test this out?

Appendix 6

Records for teenagers: My ladder

Goal	Helpful Thought	Reward
1 (EASIEST STEP)		
2		
3		
4		
5		
6		
7		
8		
9		
10 (ULTIMATE GOAL)		

Appendix 6

Records for teenagers: My ladder

Goal	Helpful Thought	Reward
1 (EASIEST STEP)		
2		
3		
4		
5		
6		
7		
8		
9		
10 (ULTIMATE GOAL)		

Records for teenagers: Problem-solving

What is the problem?	List all the possible solutions No matter how weird or wonderful	What would happen if I chose this solution? In the short term? In the long term? To my anxiety in the future?	Is this plan doable? Yes/No	How good is this plan? Rate 0–10	What happened?

Appendix 6

Records for teenagers: Problem-solving

What is the problem?	List all the possible solutions No matter how weird or wonderful	What would happen if I chose this solution? In the short term? In the long term? To my anxiety in the future?	Is this plan doable? Yes/No	How good is this plan? Rate 0–10	What happened?

Appendix 6

Records for teenagers: Social skills questionnaire

Non-verbal skills

1 Eye contact
Do you look people in the eye (without staring) when you are interacting, rather than looking down or away?

2 Posture
Do you stand or walk in a confident way, for example standing upright and walking with your head up and shoulders back?

3 Voice
Do you talk at the right volume and at the right speed? Do you talk clearly, rather than mumble?

Verbal skills

4 Greeting people
Do you say hello and goodbye to people, or do you just look down or ignore them?

5 Talking to people
Do you ask questions or say something to the other person, to start or keep a conversation going? Do you answer other people's questions and listen to what they have to say?

Friendships

6 Taking the initiative
Do you invite other teenagers to come round to your house or to go out somewhere? Do you ask if you can join in with other teenagers' activities?

7 Feelings
Do you offer to help other people if they are in trouble or need assistance? Are you kind to others who are feeling sad or upset?
Do you compliment your friends or family or praise them?

Assertiveness

8 Asking for help
Do you ask for help from adults or other teenagers if you need it?

9 Sticking up for yourself and others
Do you say 'no' if you don't want to do something that another teenager asks you to do?
Do you stick up for other children and teenagers if they need help?

10 Saying what you think
Do you say what you think, even if others might not like it, but in a way that does not upset others?

Useful books and contacts

Useful books

Adult anxiety and shyness

Butler, G., *Overcoming Social Anxiety and Shyness* (Constable and Robinson, London, 1999)
> A practical self-help book for adults with social anxiety or shyness. Uses similar techniques to the ones outlined in this book.

Kennerley, H., *Overcoming Anxiety* (Constable and Robinson, London, 1997)
> A very useful self-help book providing strategies for adults to tackle their anxiety.

Silove, D and Manicavasagar, W., *Overcoming Panic* (Constable and Robinson, London, 1997)
> A practical book designed to help adults overcome panic.

Anxiety

Creswell, C. and Willetts, L., *Overcoming Your Child's Fears and Worries: A Self-Help Guide Using Cognitive Behavioural Techniques* (Constable and Robinson, London, 2007)
> A book from the same series as this one, outlining similar strategies for helping children to overcome different types of anxiety, including phobias, worrying and separation anxiety.

Rapee, R., *Helping Your Anxious Child* (New Harbinger Publications, Oakland, CA, 2000)

A practical guide for parents which outlines a range of strategies to help anxious children, based on cognitive behavioral principles.

Bullying

Cohen-Posey, K., *How to Handle Bullies, Teasers, and Other Meanies* (Rainbow Books, USA, 1995)

A book for children, giving ideas about how to deal with bullying.

Elliott, M., *The Willow Street Kids Beat the Bullies* (Macmillan Children's Books, London, 1986)

A series of stories aimed at children aged 7–11 about a group of school friends and the situations they face during the year. Each story is based on a real incident to explain how to deal with the pressures of growing up and how to cope, avoid, overcome and recover from a variety of problems.

Elliott, M., *101 Ways to Deal with Bullying: A Guide for Parents* (Hodder Mobius, London, 1997)

This book provides strategies for tackling your child's bullying.

Elliott, M., *Wise Guides: Bullying* (Hodder Children's Books, London, 1998)

A book to help children, teenagers and parents cope with bullying. Includes chapters on assertiveness and self-esteem.

Lawson, S., *Helping Children Cope with Bullying* (Sheldon Press, London, 1994)

A guide for parents.

Selective mutism

McHolm, A.E., Cunningham, C.E. and Vanier, M.K., *Helping Your Child with Selective Mutism: Practical Steps to Overcome a Fear of Speaking* (New Harbinger Publications, Oakland, CA, 2005)

> A practical book for parents, which outlines a whole range of strategies you can use with your child in co-operation with your child's school.

Schaefer, C.E., *Cat's Got Your Tongue? A Story of Children Afraid to Speak* (Imagination Press, Washington DC, 1992)

> A book for primary school-aged children about a child who was afraid to speak, but overcame this with the help of professionals.

Shyness

Cain, B. and Smith-Moore, J.J., *I Don't Know Why… I Guess I'm Shy* (Imagination Press, Washington DC, 2000)

> A book for primary school-aged children about a boy who is shy, but manages to overcome this by using some simple coping strategies.

Hargreaves, Roger, *Little Miss Shy* (Egmont Books, London, 2003)

> For pre-school children. A great book giving children the message that if you face your fears you can overcome them and may end up enjoying yourself.

Social skills

Elman, N.M. and Kennedy-Moore, E., *The Unwritten Rules of Friendship* (Little, Brown, New York, 2003)

A book for parents outlining a broad range of strategies to use with children, including shy children, with social skills difficulties.

Krasny Brown, L. and Brown, M., *How to be a Friend* (Little, Brown, New York, 1998)

Useful contacts

UK

British Association for Behavioural and Cognitive Psychotherapies (BABCP)

Victoria Buildings

9–13 Silver Street

Bury BL9 0EU

Tel: 0161 797 4484

Website: www.babcp.org.uk

Email: babcp@babcp.com

They have a list of cognitive behavior therapists accredited by the organization.

The British Psychological Society

St Andrews House

48 Princess Road East

Leicester LE1 7DR

Tel: 0116 254 9568

Website: www.bps.org.uk

Email: enquiry@bps.org.uk

They hold a directory of chartered clinical psychologists.

Bullying Online
Windsor House
Cornwall Road
Harrogate HG1 2PW
Website: www.bullying.co.uk
Email: help@bullying.co.uk
Information and advice for children who are experiencing bullying and their parents (and children who are bullying and their parents).

Child Line
NSPCC
Weston House
42 Curtain Road
London EC2A 3NH
Tel: 0800 1111
Website: www.childline.org.uk

Parentline Plus
Website: www.parentlineplus.org.uk/
Tel: 0808 800 2222
A charity offering support and advice to anyone parenting a child.

The Royal College of Psychiatrists
17 Belgrave Square
London SW1X 8PG
Tel: 020 7235 2351
Website: www.rcpsych.ac.uk
Email: rcpsych@rcpsych.ac.uk

Contains downloadable reading materials and tapes for children and teenagers experiencing mental health problems and their parents and teachers.

YoungMinds
48–50 St John Street
London EC1M 4DG
Tel: 020 7336 8445
Website:www.youngminds.org.uk
Email:enquiries@youngminds.org.uk
A charity providing information and advice for children and teenagers experiencing mental health problems and their parents and teachers.

Specialist child anxiety clinics

Europe

Child Anxiety Clinic
and
Child Traumatic Stress Clinic
Michael Rutter Centre
Maudsley Hospital
Denmark Hill
London SE5 8AZ
Tel: 0203 228 3381
Fax: 0203 228 5011
Accepts national referrals for assessment and treatment.

The University of Reading Child Anxiety Research Clinic

Dr Lucy Willetts

School of Psychology

University of Reading

3 Craven Road

Reading

Berkshire RG1 5LF

Accepts referrals from across Berkshire for assessment and treatment.

European Association for Behavioural and Cognitive Therapies (EABCT)

Website: www.eabct.com

Provides links to national cognitive therapy organizations in Europe. It lists, for example, the website for the Netherlands Association of Behaviour and Cognitive Therapy (which keeps a register of cognitive therapists). Website: www.vgct.nl

Other useful resources

Australia

FRIENDS for life

Website: www.friendsinfo.net

Information on a school-based prevention and treatment program for anxious children and young people. Includes downloadable materials for school personnel.

Macquarie University Anxiety Research Unit (MUARU)
Ronald M. Rapee, PhD, Director
Macquarie University
Sydney NSW 2109
Tel: 00 612 02 9850 8711
Website: www.psy.mq.edu.au/MUARU/
Information, assessment and treatment for children, teenagers and adults with anxiety disorders.

USA

Academy of Cognitive Therapy
One Belmont Avenue
Suite 700
Bala Cynwyd PA 19004–1610
Tel: 00 1 610 664 1273
Website: www.academyofct.org
Email: info@academyofct.org
Lists accredited cognitive therapists in the USA and other countries.

American Psychiatric Association
1000 Wilson Boulevard
Suite 1825
Arlington VA 22209–3901
Website: www.psych.org
Email: apa@psych.org
Tel: 00 1 703 907 7300
Provides resources for the public on www.healthyminds.org.

American Psychological Society
750 First Street
NE
Washington DC 20002-4242
Tel: 00 1 800 374 2721 or 00 1 202 336 5500
Website: www.apa.org
Keeps a register of psychologists.

Anxiety Disorders Association of America
Website: www.adaa.org
Information on anxiety disorders, including a focus on children and young people.

Association for Behavioral and Cognitive Therapies (ABCT)
305 Seventh Avenue
16th Floor
New York NY 10001
Tel: 00 1 212 647 1890
Website: www.aabt.org
Keeps a directory of cognitive and behavior therapists.

Beck Institute for Cognitive Therapy and Research
One Belmont Avenue
Suite 700
Bala Cynwyd PA 19004-1610
Tel: 00 1 610 664 3020
Website: www.beckinstitute.org
Information, treatment and training provided.

The International Society for Traumatic Stress Studies (ISTSS)
60 Revere Drive
Suite 500
Northbrook IL 60062
Tel: 00 1 847 480 9028
Website: www.istss.org/index.cfm
E-mail: istss@istss.org
Resources and links relating to stress following a traumatic event.

The Child Anxiety NETWORK
Website: www.childanxiety.net
Information, resources and list of healthcare providers specializing in treatment of child anxiety.

WorryWiseKids.org
Website: www.worrywisekids.org
Information for parents

Index

Index

Order further books in the *Overcoming* series

Qnty	Title	RRP	Offer price	Total
	Bulimia Nervosa and Binge-Eating	£9.99	£7.99	
	Overcoming Anger and Irritability	£9.99	£7.99	
	Overcoming Anorexia Nervosa	£9.99	£7.99	
	Overcoming Anxiety	£9.99	£7.99	
	Overcoming Anxiety Self-Help Course (3 parts)	£21.00	£15.00	
	Overcoming Bulimia Nervosa and Binge-Eating Self-Help Course (3 parts)	£21.00	£15.00	
	Overcoming Childhood Trauma	£9.99	£7.99	
	Overcoming Chronic Fatigue	£9.99	£7.99	
	Overcoming Chronic Pain	£9.99	£7.99	
	Overcoming Compulsive Gambling	£9.99	£7.99	
	Overcoming Depersonalization and Feelings of Unreality	£9.99	£9.99	
	Overcoming Depression	£9.99	£7.99	
	Overcoming Insomnia and Sleep Problems	£9.99	£7.99	
	Overcoming Low Self-Esteem	£9.99	£7.99	
	Overcoming Low Self-Esteem Self-Help Course (3 parts)	£21.00	£15.00	
	Overcoming Mood Swings	£9.99	£7.99	
	Overcoming Obsessive Compulsive Disorders	£9.99	£7.99	
	Overcoming Panic	£9.99	£7.99	
	Overcoming Panic and Agoraphobia Self-Help Course (3 parts)	£21.00	£15.00	
	Overcoming Paranoid and Suspicious Thoughts	£9.99	£7.99	
	Overcoming Problem Drinking	£9.99	£7.99	
	Overcoming Relationship Problems	£9.99	£7.99	
	Overcoming Sexual Problems	£9.99	£7.99	
	Overcoming Social Anxiety and Shyness	£9.99	£7.99	
	Overcoming Social Anxiety and Shyness Self-Help Course (3 parts)	£21.00	£15.00	
	Overcoming Traumatic Stress	£9.99	£7.99	
	Overcoming Weight Problems	£9.99	£7.99	
	Overcoming Your Child's Fears and Worries	£9.99	£7.99	
	Overcoming Your Smoking Habit	£9.99	£7.99	
	Manage Your Mood	£12.99	£10.99	
	P&P		**FREE**	**FREE**
	TOTAL			

Name: _____

Address: _____

_____ Postcode: _____

Daytime Tel. No.: _____

Email: _____

(in case of query)

How to pay:

1. **By telephone**: call the TBS order line on 01206 255 800 and quote **SHY**. Phone lines are open between Monday–Friday, 8.30am–5.30pm.

2. **By post**: send a cheque for the full amount payable to TBS Ltd. or if paying by debit, credit or Switch card, fill in the details below and send the form to:
Freepost RLUL-SJGC-SGKJ, Cash Sales/Direct Mail Dept., The Book Service, Colchester Road, Frating, Colchester CO7 7DW.